Pocket LAS VEGAS

TOP SIGHTS · LOCAL LIFE · MADE EASY

D1005486

Andrea Schulte-Peevers, Benedict Walker

In This Book

QuickStart Guide

Your keys to understanding the city – we help you decide what to do and how to do it

Need to Know
Tips for a smooth trip

Neighborhoods
What's where

Explore Las Vegas

The best things to see and do, neighborhood by neighborhood

Top Sights
Make the most of your visit

Local Life
The insider's city

The Best of Las Vegas

The city's highlights in handy lists to help you plan

Best Walks
See the city on foot

Las Vegas' Best...
The best experiences

Survival Guide

Tips and tricks for a seamless, hassle-free city experience

Getting Around
Travel like a local

Essential Information
Including where to stay

Our selection of the city's best places to eat, drink and experience:

◎ **Sights**

✖ **Eating**

🍷 **Drinking**

✦ **Entertainment**

🔒 **Shopping**

These symbols give you the vital information for each listing:

☎ Telephone Numbers	👪 Family-Friendly
☉ Opening Hours	🐾 Pet-Friendly
Ⓟ Parking	🚌 Bus
⊖ Nonsmoking	⛴ Ferry
@ Internet Access	Ⓜ Metro
🛜 Wi-Fi Access	🚝 Monorail
🥗 Vegetarian Selection	Ⓢ Subway
📖 English-Language Menu	🚋 Tram
	🚆 Train

Find each listing quickly on maps for each neighborhood:

Bar Hemingway

16 🍷 Map p233, B2

Legend has it that Hemi self, wielding a machine rate this timber-pan ered bar during showpiece is a en by Papa ar town. Dress s.com; Hôtel Rit ☉6.30pm-2a

Lonely Planet's Las Vegas

Lonely Planet Pocket Guides are designed to get you straight to the heart of the city.

Inside you'll find all the must-see sights, plus tips to make your visit to each one really memorable. We've split the city into easy-to-navigate neighborhoods and provided clear maps so you'll find your way around with ease. Our expert authors have searched out the best of the city: walks, food, nightlife and shopping, to name a few. Because you want to explore, our 'Local Life' pages will take you to some of the most exciting areas to experience the real Las Vegas.

And of course you'll find all the practical tips you need for a smooth trip: itineraries for short visits, how to get around, and how much to tip the guy who serves you a drink at the end of a long day's exploration.

It's your guarantee of a really great experience.

Our Promise

You can trust our travel information because Lonely Planet authors visit the places we write about, each and every edition. We never accept freebies for positive coverage, so you can rely on us to tell it like it is.

QuickStart Guide 7

Las Vegas Top Sights............8
Las Vegas Day Planner......12
Need to Know....................14
Las Vegas
Neighborhoods..................16

Explore Las Vegas 19

20 The Strip

74 East of the Strip

88 West of the Strip

98 Downtown &
Fremont Street

Worth a Trip:

Grand Canyon....................116
Hoover Dam & Lake Mead............120

The Best of Las Vegas   125

Las Vegas' Best Walks

The Center Strip 126
Downtown 128

Las Vegas' Best ...

Buffets 130
Architecture 131
Shopping 132
Nightlife 134
Casinos 136
Live Entertainment 138
Fine Dining 140
Local Culture 142
Off-Strip Dining 144
For Newlyweds 145
For Kids 146

Survival Guide   147

Before You Go 148
Arriving in Las Vegas 150
Getting Around 150
Essential Information 152

QuickStart Guide

Las Vegas Top Sights 8

Las Vegas Day Planner 12

Need to Know 14

Las Vegas Neighborhoods 16

Welcome to Las Vegas

Vegas, baby! An oasis of indulgence dazzling in the desert. The Strip shimmers hypnotically, promising excitement, entertainment, fortune and fame. Where else can you spend the night partying in ancient Rome, wake up for brunch beneath the Eiffel Tower, watch an erupting volcano at sunset and get married in a pink Cadillac? All in Sin City. It's yours for the taking.

The Venetian (p44)
DUANE WALKER/GETTY IMAGES ©

Las Vegas
Top Sights

Golden Nugget
(p100)

Downtown's classiest old-school casino haunt.

Bellagio (p22)

The Strip's original opulent palazzo.

Mob Museum
(p102)

Where Las Vegas began.

Wynn & Encore
(p48)

The Strip's sassiest trendsetting twins.

New York–New York (p30)

Las Vegas' little Big Apple.

LINQ Promenade (p34)

Outdoor shopping-dining-drinking fun.

National Atomic Testing Museum (p80)

Mushroom clouds over the desert. (Geiger counters)

Mandalay Bay (p27)

The Mojave's ultimate 'tropical' oasis.

CityCenter (p36)

Amazing Aria. Classy Cosmo. Crystals.

Paris Las Vegas (p40)

Paris in the desert.

TRAVELVIEW/SHUTTERSTOCK ©

COURTESY OF THE SPRINGS PRESERVE ©

Venetian & Palazzo (p44)

A little slice of Italy.

Springs Preserve (p90)

A real-life desert oasis.

Las Vegas
Day Planner

Day One

Start your day by taking a peek or renting a cabana at **Mandalay Bay Beach** (p27). Explore the casino and get your bearings: you might return for classy cocktails at **Skyfall Lounge** (p27) or French fine dining at **Rivea** (p62). Walk north past **Luxor** (p57) to the streets of **New York–New York** (p30) and take a selfie with Lady Liberty, then duck into classy **Cosmopolitan** (p37) to gawk at its mind-blowing lobby – but be quick, or you won't make it to **Paris** (p40) for lunch with views of the **Fountains of Bellagio** (p23).

Follow the signs for the Bally's & Paris Monorail station and ride one stop. Walk north beneath the track to the unmissable **High Roller** (p35). Take a ride, or turn left and walk the length of the fun **LINQ Promenade** (p34). If you fancy a first flutter, try **LINQ** (p54), or if you prefer pink, the **Flamingo** (p57). Cross the street to **Caesars Palace** (p54) for dinner and a show.

After dinner, hit **Drai's** (p67) (atop Cromwell, opposite), if you're game and appropriately attired. Tip: swap walking between stops with rides on the Deuce/SDX buses.

Day Two

Head to **Aria** (p37) to admire the eclectic **CityCenter fine art collection** (p37). Pop next door to the **Shops at Crystals** (p71) or head back to **Cosmopolitan** (p37) to further explore this playground of the nouveau riches. Take note of the **Chandelier Lounge** (p68) for cocktails later...or have one now. Walk north past **Paris Las Vegas** (p40) and the **Venetian** (p44) to the latter's sophisticated little sister, **Palazzo** (p44).

Continue north, walking across the skybridge to Steve Wynn's signature showpiece, **Wynn** (p48). Stroll through the sumptuous atrium, perhaps stopping at the whimsical **Parasol Up & Parasol Down** (p50) lounge to gaze upon the Lake of Dreams, then cross the opulent casino floor to **Encore** (p48) and check with the concierge for last-minute tickets to Cirque du Soleil's underwater masterpiece, **Le Rêve the Dream** (p49).

Grab a taxi/rideshare to **Stratosphere** (p54) for cocktails-with-a-view at **107 SkyLounge** (p66).

Short on time?
We've arranged Las Vegas' must-sees into these day-by-day itineraries to make sure you see the very best of the city in the time you have available.

Day Three

☀ Head to the western corner of N Las Vegas Blvd and Fremont St to begin your exploration of Downtown Las Vegas, where it all began. Ride the **Slotzilla** (p111) zipline (if you're game) or walk the length of Fremont St to the iconic **Golden Nugget** (p100) with its famous shark tank and the largest gold nugget ever found. Opposite, you'll find antique **Binion's** (p110) – a must for Elvis fans! Continue one block north to Stewart Ave and the excellent **Mob Museum** (p102) to learn how the Mafia shaped Sin City.

☀ Grab a taxi/rideshare up the street to the **Neon Museum** (p109) (resist the temptation to walk – it's not the best part of town). When you're done, head to the **Burlesque Hall of Fame** (p111), then get a shot of **El Cortez** (p111), opposite, and continue a block east to the quirky **Container Park** (p105).

☾ The bars of Fremont East await: kick off at the speakeasy-style **Downtown Cocktail Room** (p114), hipster-haven **Beauty Bar** (p105) or on the rooftop patio at Prohibition-era-inspired **Commonwealth** (p105).

Day Four

☀ You've hit the Strip and done Downtown, so what else is in Vegas? Lots! Start by heading west of the Strip to family-friendly **Springs Preserve** (p90) to explore Sin City's natural and cultural side, then head south to the **Rio** (p94) to scream your head off while wooshing 400ft in the air on the **VooDoo Zipline** (p94). Stay at the Rio to gorge yourself at the **Carnival World Buffet** (p96) or join the locals for noodle soups or barbecue at nearby **Chinatown Plaza** (p96).

☀ Head east of the Strip for a spin around the eerily fascinating **National Atomic Testing Museum** (p80) to learn about the days when atomic bomb explosions were considered a tourist attraction. More kooky sightseeing? Work a trip to the **Pinball Hall of Fame** (p84) into your schedule, or, head to **Firefly** (p85) for happy hour drinks.

☾ Steer the compass to the hippest hotel east of the Strip – the **Hard Rock Hotel & Casino** (p76). Ogle the rock-and-roll memorabilia before reporting for dinner duty at **Culinary Dropout** (p77). Afterwards, hit the show at the **Joint** (p87) or get a dose of hilarious madness at the **Double Down Saloon** (p86).

Need to Know

**For more information,
see Survival Guide (p147)**

Currency
US dollar ($)

Language
English

Visas
Not usually required for citizens of Canada or the 37 Visa Waiver Program countries with ESTA pre-authorization.

Money
ATM transaction fees inside casino gaming areas are high. Credit cards are widely accepted.

Cell Phones
Cell (mobile) phones must be a multiband GSM model.

Time
Pacific Time Zone (GMT/UTC minus eight hours)

Tipping
The standard tip is 18% to 20% of the bill. If a service charge has already been included (usually for groups of six or more), don't tip twice. At buffets, leave a couple of dollars per person on the table.

① Before You Go

Your Daily Budget

Budget: Less than $100
▶ Downtown casino hotel room: $30–80
▶ Takeout meal: $6–12
▶ 24-hour RTC bus pass: $8

Midrange: $100–250
▶ Standard Strip casino hotel room: $65–150
▶ Discounted show ticket: $30–90
▶ Casual restaurant meal: $20–45
▶ 24-hour self parking at a Strip hotel: $10–15

Top end: More than $250
▶ Luxury Strip hotel suite: $200-plus
▶ VIP show ticket: $125-plus
▶ Celebrity-chef dining: $100-plus

Useful Websites

Lonely Planet (www.lonelyplanet.com/usa/las-vegas) Destination information, hotel bookings, traveler forum and more.

Las Vegas Tourism (www.lasvegastourism.com) Official website of Las Vegas Tourism.

Las Vegas Weekly (www.lasvegasweekly.com) Popular weekly magazine with listings, in print and online.

Advance Planning

One month before Book flights, a hotel and a rental car for trips out of town.

Three weeks before Score tickets for production shows, mega-concerts or headliner events.

One week before Book a table at a happening chef's restaurant or an outdoor adventure tour.

② Arriving in Las Vegas

Most travelers arrive in Las Vegas by car or by plane. The airport is located relatively close to the Strip. Shuttle buses depart for casino-hotels around the clock, and taxis are readily available.

✈ McCarran International Airport

McCarran offers free wi-fi and gadget-recharging workstations; ATMs, a currency exchange booth and full-service bank; first-aid and police stations; a pharmacy and walk-in medical clinic for nonemergencies; a lost-and-found office; a post office; and tourist information desks.

Shuttle buses run to Strip hotels from $7 one-way, and from $9 to Downtown and off-Strip hotels. You'll pay at least $20 plus tip for a taxi to the Strip – tell your driver to use surface streets, not the I-15 Fwy airport connector tunnel ('long-hauling').

🚌 Greyhound Terminal

If you're arriving in Vegas via long-distance bus, you'll disembark at a downtown station just off the Fremont Street Experience. To reach the Strip, catch a southbound SDX bus.

🚗 Driving

Most travelers approach the Strip (Las Vegas Blvd) off the I-15 Fwy. Try to avoid exiting onto busy Flamingo Rd; opt for quieter Tropicana Ave or Spring Mountain Rd.

③ Getting Around

The Strip is miles long. Though you can walk between some casino resorts, you'll need a ride – bus, monorail, taxi or driving your own car – to reach others, or to go downtown.

🚌 Bus

Deuce buses to/from downtown stop every block or two along the Strip. Quicker SDX express buses stop at some Strip casino hotels and at some off-Strip shopping malls. A 24-hour pass costs $8.

🚗 Car & Motorcycle

Driving on the Strip can be stressful. Parking at Strip casino hotels and shopping malls is no longer free.

🚝 Monorail

Expensive, inconveniently located on the east side of the Strip and with a limited route, but has great views and regular services.

🚗 Rideshare

Uber and Lyft are by far the best way to get around Vegas in most circumstances, and even cheaper when traveling with others.

🚌 Shuttle

Many off-Strip casino hotels offer limited free shuttle buses to and from the Strip, although some are reserved for hotel guests. A free public shuttle connects the Rio with Harrah's and Bally's/Paris Las Vegas.

🚗 Taxi

It's illegal to hail a cab but there are taxi stands at almost every casino hotel and shopping mall. Rides cost at least $20, plus tip.

🚊 Tram

Free air-conditioned trams operate on three routes: one connects the Bellagio, CityCenter and the Monte Carlo; another links Treasure Island and the Mirage, while a third travels between Excalibur, Luxor and Mandalay Bay.

Las Vegas
Neighborhoods

West of the Strip (p88)

A pair of popular casino hotels, one of the city's best buffets, desert gardens, natural history exhibits and Vegas' very own Chinatown.

◉ Top Sights

Springs Preserve

Springs
◉ Preserve

The Strip (p20)

Flashy megaresorts and glowing neon signs line 4.5 miles of famed Las Vegas Blvd.

◉ Top Sights

Bellagio

Mandalay Bay

New York–New York

LINQ Promenade

CityCenter

Paris Las Vegas

Venetian & Palazzo

Wynn & Encore

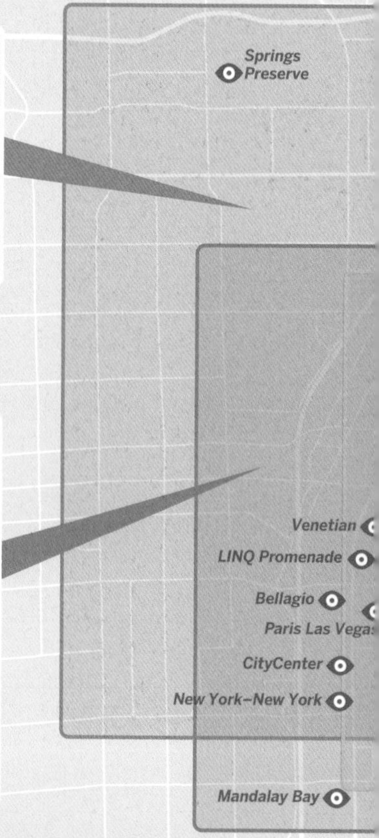

Venetian ◉

LINQ Promenade ◉

Bellagio ◉

Paris Las Vegas

CityCenter ◉

New York–New York ◉

Mandalay Bay ◉

Mob Museum

Golden Nugget

Downtown & Fremont St (p98)
Vintage Vegas vibes, old-school casinos, excellent new museums and a burgeoning hipster nightlife scene in Sin City's downtown.

Top Sights

Golden Nugget

Mob Museum

Wynn & Encore

National Atomic Testing Museum

Hard Rock

East of the Strip (p74)
Quirky special-interest museums, university bars, secondhand shopping and a perennially cool rock 'n' roll–themed resort.

Top Sights

Hard Rock Hotel & Casino

National Atomic Testing Museum

Explore
Las Vegas

The Strip 20

East of the Strip 74

West of the Strip 88

Downtown & Fremont Street 98

Worth a Trip
Grand Canyon 116
Hoover Dam & Lake Mead...................... 120

Paris Las Vegas (p40) and the Strip at night
F11PHOTO/SHUTTERSTOCK ©

Explore

The Strip

The 4.2-mile Strip (a section of S Las Vegas Blvd) is what happens when you take the ideals of freedom and abundance to their extremes. It's Vegas' entertainment central, the epicenter in a vortex of limitless potential, where almost anything goes and time becomes elastic.

The Sights in a Day

Take in the famous **Fountains of Bellagio** (p23) show, then step inside the resort to admire Dale Chihuly's glass sculpture and the lavish landscaping inside the **Bellagio Conservatory & Botanical Gardens** (p23). Stop for coffee and chocolates at **Jean Philippe Patisserie** (p24). Diehard Francophiles should detour south to ascend the **Eiffel Tower** (p41) at Paris Las Vegas.

Head north toward **Caesars Palace** (p54) to see the opulent Greco-Roman–inspired casino. Walk through the **Forum Shops** (p72), stopping for a spiked lemonade outside at the Spanish Steps. Watch the exploding **volcano** (p57) outside the Mirage, then cross the Strip to see the floating gondolas outside the palatial **Venetian** (p44). Cap a shopping spree at the **Grand Canal Shoppes** (p46) with an early Latin-Japanese dinner at **Sushisamba** (p45) at sister property **Palazzo** (p44).

Return to the Mirage to catch Cirque du Soleil's show **Beatles LOVE** (p68). Grab alfresco drinks at **Rhumbar** (p126), or take a cab down to Mandalay Bay and ride the elevator to elegant Skyfall Lounge atop the Delano for unparalleled views of the glittering southern Strip.

 Top Sights

Bellagio (p22)

Mandalay Bay (p26)

New York–New York (p30)

LINQ Promenade (p34)

CityCenter (p36)

Paris Las Vegas (p40)

Venetian & Palazzo (p44)

Wynn & Encore (p48)

 Best of Las Vegas

Fine Dining

Eiffel Tower Restaurant (p41)

Rivea (p62)

Restaurant Guy Savoy (p60)

Bars

Chandelier Lounge (p68)

Skyfall Lounge (p27)

Beer Park (p41)

Getting There

🚌 **Bus** Shuttle buses run from the airport to resorts on the Strip. From downtown, take the Deuce & SDX.

🚕 **Taxi** $15 to $25 plus tip from either the airport or Downtown.

Top Sights
Bellagio

Inspired by the beauty of a lakeside Italian village, casino magnate Steve Wynn's original Vegas pleasure palazzo, with its ornate Tuscan architecture and artificial lake, anchors the center Strip. A thousand dancing fountains spring from the lake's waters and, while its overt opulence can be too much for some, Bellagio's secret delight is that romance is always in the air.

👁 Map p52, B5

📞 888-987-6667

www.bellagio.com

3600 S Las Vegas Blvd

🕐 24hr

P 🐾

Fountains of Bellagio

Fountains of Bellagio

Out of the faux Italian lake spring the dancing **Fountains of Bellagio** (www.bellagio.com; Bellagio; admission free; ☺shows every 30min 3-8pm Mon-Fri, noon-8pm Sat, 11am-7pm Sun, every 15min 8pm-midnight Mon-Sat, from 7pm Sun; P♿), every 15 to 30 minutes throughout the afternoon and evening. The recorded soundtrack varies; if you're lucky, it'll be Italian opera or ol' Blue Eyes crooning 'Luck Be a Lady.' For front-row seats, head to **Hyde** (☎702-693-8700; www.hydebellagio.com; cover $20-40, usually free before 10pm; ☺lounge 5-11pm daily, nightclub 10pm-4am Tue, Fri & Sat) for happy hour and lean over the balcony to almost feel the spray, or reserve an outdoor patio table at one of Bellagio's lakefront restaurants. Afterward, stroll over to Jean Philippe Patisserie (p24), just so you can say you've seen the world's largest chocolate fountain up close.

Lobby

The hotel's gasp-worthy lobby has an 18ft-high ceiling adorned with a backlit glass sculpture by Dale Chihuly, comprised of 2000 hand-blown flowers in vibrant colors. It's especially lovely to behold when someone is playing the grand piano at the nearby **Petrossian Bar** (☎702-693-7111; ☺24hr).

Bellagio Conservatory & Botanical Gardens

At the **Bellagio Conservatory & Botanical Gardens** (admission free; ☺24hr; P♿), ostentatious seasonal floral arrangements are installed by cranes through the soaring 50ft ceiling. The effect is unnatural, but that doesn't stop crowds from gawking – and the aroma of fresh blooms is truly enchanting. Real flowers, cultivated in a gigantic on-site greenhouse, brighten countless vases throughout the property. Also around the periphery of the conservatory are classic paintings

---

☑ Top Tips

▶ For the best photo ops of the famous Conservatory, come by in the early morning.

▶ Checking in? Splurge on a fountain-view room.

▶ Unaccompanied children under 18 are not allowed at the Bellagio. Baby strollers are prohibited except for use by hotel guests.

✖ Take a Break

To enjoy the spectacle of the Fountains of Bellagio over a cold beer, head to Beer Park (by Budweiser; p41).

If you want fine dining with your fountains, set your sights high upon the Eiffel Tower Restaurant (p41), or, to get really up-close-and-personal, Todd English's Olives (p64).

recreated with buds and blooms instead of oil paint.

Bellagio Gallery of Fine Art

Since Steve Wynn sold his baby to the MGM Grand group for $6.4 billion, Bellagio hasn't been blessed with the same world-class art. Yet its petite **fine arts gallery** (☎702-693-7871; adult/child under 12yr $18/free; ☺10am-8pm, last entry 7:30pm; ❙Ｐ❙❙♿❙) still hosts such blockbuster traveling shows as Claude Monet: Impressions of Light and American Modernism from the Museum of Fine Arts, Boston. Original modern art masterworks hang inside (☎702-693-8865; prix-fixe dinner menus without/with wine pairings $119/179; ☺5:30-9:30pm Wed-Mon; ❙🍴❙) restaurant, nearby.

Understand
Steve Wynn's Vision

Steve Wynn dreamed up the $1.6 billion Bellagio, adorned with $300 million worth of art from his personal collection of masterpieces. Built on the ashes of the demolished 1950s-era Dunes, Bellagio was one of the world's most opulent casino hotels when it opened in 1998. It also brought a surprising touch of elegance to Sin City, which had become infamous for its down-and-dirty strip clubs and low-class culture. Wynn sold the Mirage and Bellagio megaresorts to business rival MGM Grand in 2000.

Pool Complex

Sprawling behind the hotel, Bellagio's lushly landscaped five-pool complex evokes the Mediterranean. As only hotel guests are able to experience it, and no unaccompanied children under 14 years old are allowed, it's also a relatively tranquil pool scene for Vegas. To unwind even more, hotel guests can book rejuvenating treatments at **Spa Bellagio** (☎702-693-7472; guests/nonguests day pass $40/50; ☺6am-8pm).

Cirque du Soleil's 'O'

Phonetically speaking, it's the French word for water *(eau)*. With a lithe international cast performing in, on and above water, **O** (☎888-488-7111; www.cirquedusoleil.com; tickets $99-185; ☺7pm & 9:30pm Wed-Sun) is a spectacular feat of imagination and engineering, and you'll pay dearly to see it – the company never sells discounted tickets.

Jean Philippe Patisserie

As certified by the *Guinness Book of World Records,* the world's largest chocolate fountain cascades inside the front windows of this champion **pastry-maker's shop** (www.jpchocolates.com; snacks & drinks $4-11; ☺6am-11pm Mon-Thu, to midnight Fri-Sun; ❙♿❙), known for its fantastic sorbets, gelati, pastries and chocolate confections. Coffee and espresso are above the Strip's low-bar average.

BELLAGIO

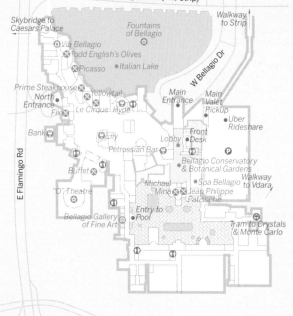

Skybridge to Bally's

S Las Vegas Blvd (The Strip)

Skybridge to
Caesars Palace

Walkway
to Strip

Via Bellagio
Todd English's Olives

Fountains
of Bellagio

W Bellagio Dr

Picasso

Italian Lake

Prime Steakhouse
North
Entrance
Fix

Yellowtail

Le Cirque Hyde

Main
Entrance

Main
Valet
Pickup

Uber
Rideshare

Bank

Lily

Front
Desk

Petrossian Bar

Lobby

Bellagio Conservatory
& Botanical Gardens

Buffet

Michael
Mina

Spa Bellagio

Walkway
to Vdara

Jean Philippe
Patisserie

"O" Theatre

Entry to
Pool

Bellagio Gallery
of Fine Art

Tram to Crystals
& Monte Carlo

E Flamingo Rd

Top Sights
Mandalay Bay

Angular and glittering gold, massive Mandalay Bay flanks the far south end of the Strip. It's the first resort many visitors lay eyes on as they roll into Las Vegas – and what better introduction to Sin City than this gleaming tropics-in-the-desert–themed, high-rise shrine to casino gaming and high-rolling, with its massive beach, aquarium, exceptional dining and two luxe hotels-within-a-hotel.

Map p52, B8

702-632-7700

www.mandalaybay.com

3950 S Las Vegas Blvd

24hr

Mandalay Bay Beach

The 1.6-million-gallon wave pool at **Mandalay Bay Beach** (📞877-632-7800; www.mandalaybay.com/en/amenities/beach.html; ⊙pool 8am-5pm, Moorea Beach Club 11am-6pm; 🚼) occupies 11 acres, has 2700 tons of imported Californian sand and can generate waves up to 6ft. The facility also includes a lazy river (kids love it) and the 'toptional' adults-only Moorea Beach Club. Access is complimentary to resort guests. Nonguests can enjoy the facilities by renting a reserved seat ($50 to $75 daily), daybed (from $225) or cabana ($300 to $600); daybeds and cabanas can be used by four to 10 people.

Skyfall Lounge

One of M-Bay's lesser-known draw-cards is the fabulous, dress-to-impress **Skyfall Lounge** (📞702-632-7575; www.delanolasvegas.com; Delano; ⊙5pm-midnight Sun-Thu, to 1:30am Fri & Sat), atop the Delano hotel, from where you can enjoy unparalleled views of the southern Strip and sip cocktails as the sun sets over the spectacular Spring Mountains. The bar's classy, subdued vibe becomes ever so slightly more tactile when top DJs start spinning mellow beats after dark and the more self-assured (or inebriated) guests get primed to dance the night away.

Shark Reef Aquarium

Adults, kids and lovers of marine life flock to Mandalay Bay for its unique and unusual walk-through **Shark Reef Aquarium** (📞702-632-4555; www.sharkreef.com; 3950 S Las Vegas Blvd; adult/child $25/19; ⊙10am-8pm Sun-Thu, to 10pm Fri & Sat; **P** 🚼). Here you'll find around 2000 species of submarine critters, including jellyfish, moray eels, stingrays and, of course, several species of shark. Also on display are some of the world's last remaining

☑ Top Tips

▶ Free trams shuttle between Mandalay Bay and the Luxor and Excalibur casino hotels.

▶ Pick up tickets for an outdoor concert by the Mandalay Bay Beach swimming pool at the Mandalay Bay Events Center (p28).

▶ Shop around for discounted tickets to *Michael Jackson ONE* (p28) – bargains can be found.

✕ Take a Break

Take a stroll through the airy **Shoppes at Mandalay Place** (📞702-632-7700; www.mandalay-bay.com; Mandalay Bay; ⊙10am-11pm) promenade for coffee and window-shopping.

If it's hot outside, cool off with icy cocktails inside **Minus5 Ice Bar** (📞702-740-5800; www.minus5experience.com; Shoppes at Mandalay Bay; entry with parka, gloves & boot rental $19, incl 2 cocktails $39; ⊙11am-2am Sun-Thu, to 3am Fri & Sat).

> ## Understand
> ### The History of M-Bay
>
> The 1950s-era Hacienda resort was imploded in 1996 to clear the way for Mandalay Bay. The resort's upscale tropical theme may be subtle, but its grand opening – during which Jim Belushi, Dan Aykroyd and John Goodman cruised through the front doors on motorcycles – certainly wasn't. Today, a Harley-Davidson crew might look out of place in the regal, ivory-hued lobby.

golden crocodiles. Scuba-diver caretakers and naturalists are available to chat as you wander around.

Michael Jackson ONE

Disco babes flock to M-Bay to relive their favorite moments from the 'King of Pop's' almost 40-year career at Cirque du Soleil's musical homage to this peerless legend, *Michael Jackson ONE* (🖉702-632-7580; www.cirquedusoleil. com; tickets from $69; ⏲7pm & 9:30pm Fri-Tue). Featuring showstopping dancers, lissome acrobats and aerialists all moving to a soundtrack of MJ's greatest hits, the show moon-walks all the way back to his break-out platinum album, *Thriller*. No children under five years old allowed. You don't have to stay at the Bay to see the show, but it sure adds another great reason to, if you needed further persuasion.

House of Blues

In the **House of Blues** (🖉702-632-7600; www.houseofblues.com; ⏲box office 9am-9pm), the sophisticated **Foundation Room** (🖉702-632-7601; www.houseofblues. com; cover usually $30; ⏲5pm-2am)

nightclub hosts nightly DJ parties and special events in a stylish space that's half Gothic mansion, half Hindu temple. The expansive views of the Strip are as impressive as the decor. Look for club promoters around the casino passing out two-for-one drink and free-entry tickets. But if clubbing's not your bag, perhaps the legendary **House of Blues Gospel Brunch** (🖉702-632-7600; www.houseofblues.com; adult/child under 11yr $50/27; ⏲seatings 10am & 1pm Sun; 👪) on Sundays will be. Here, Saturday-night sinners can find redemption over unlimited Bloody Marys and Southern and soul-food favorites such as jambalaya, chicken and waffles, jalapeño cornbread and warm banana-bread pudding. Mmm-mmmm!

Mandalay Bay Events Center

Operatic tenor Luciano Pavarotti performed at the opening of this arena-style **events center** (🖉702-632-7777; www.mandalaybay.com; ⏲box office 10am-6pm), which hosts championship boxing, ultimate fighting and headliner concerts from Journey to Lady Antebellum.

MANDALAY BAY

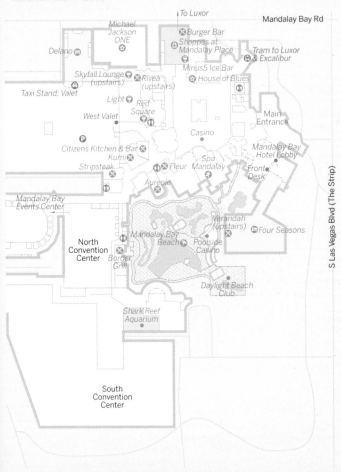

To Luxor

Mandalay Bay Rd

Michael Jackson ONE

Burger Bar

Shoppes at Mandalay Place

Delano

Tram to Luxor & Excalibur

Minus5 Ice Bar

Skyfall Lounge (upstairs)

Rivea (upstairs)

House of Blues

Taxi Stand; Valet

Light

Red Square

West Valet

Casino

Main Entrance

Mandalay Bay Hotel Lobby

Citizens Kitchen & Bar

Kumi

Spa Mandalay

Front Desk

Stripsteak

Fleur

Aureole

Mandalay Bay Events Center

Verandah (upstairs)

Four Seasons

North Convention Center

Mandalay Bay Beach

Poolside Casino

Border Grill

Daylight Beach Club

Shark Reef Aquarium

South Convention Center

S Las Vegas Blvd (The Strip)

Top Sights
New York–New York

Make no mistake: with its miniature replica skyline and themed bars, this casino-resort is nothing like the Big Apple – except for the fact that, like its namesake, it isn't exactly wholesome. Still, the Vegas version, with its eye-catching monuments such as a pint-sized Statue of Liberty, a scaled-down Brooklyn Bridge and a Coney Island–style roller coaster, is good-spirited fun.

Map p52, C7

800-689-1797

www.newyorknewyork.com

3790 S Las Vegas Blvd

24hr

P

NYC-Inspired Architecture

The mini-megalopolis of New York–New York features scaled-down replicas of the Big Apple's landmarks, such as the Statue of Liberty and a miniature Brooklyn Bridge out front. Rising above are perspective-warping replicas of the Chrysler, Empire State and Bankers Trust buildings. Inside, don't overlook the bas-relief map of the USA or Greenwich Village's cobblestone streets.

Big Apple Arcade & Roller Coaster

The gargantuan **Big Apple Arcade** (☉8am-midnight; P ♿) boasts 200-plus video games ranging from '80s classics to the latest Japanese imports. It leads out to the Coney Island–inspired **Roller Coaster** (☎702-740-6616; single ride/day pass $15/26; ☉11am-11pm Sun-Thu, 10:30am-midnight Fri & Sat; P ♿), ridden by more than a million people each year and known for its twist-and-dive maneuver, which produces a sensation similar to that a fighter pilot feels during a barrel roll. The rest of the three-minute trip includes stomach-dropping dips, high-banked turns, a 180-degree spiral and blink-and-you'll-miss-it views of the Strip. Hold on tight: your head, back and shoulders will take a beating on this bumpy ride.

Nine Fine Irishmen

Built in Ireland and shipped piece by piece to America, the **Nine Fine Irishmen** (☎702-740-6463; www.ninefineirishmen.com; ☉11am-11pm, live music from 9pm; 🛜) pub has cavernous interior booths and outdoor patio tables beside the Brooklyn Bridge. Live entertainment is a mix of Celtic rock and traditional Irish country tunes, occasionally with sing-alongs and a champion Irish dancer. Dig into finessed country cooking from this decent (though pricey) menu of lamb stew, bangers and mash, corned-beef sandwiches and other pub grub, washed down with pints of Guinness.

☑ Top Tips

▶ The crowd here is generally young and party-hearty, not Upper East Side–elegant.

▶ The roller coaster is especially exhilarating at night: the ride stays open until 11pm Sunday through Thursday, and until midnight on weekends.

▶ Staying the night? These digs are decent, but rather tiny (just what one would expect in NYC) – best for fun-loving budget travelers.

✖ Take a Break

Bar at Times Square (☎702-740-6466; New York–New York; cover $10-25, free until 7pm; ☉1pm-2:30am Mon-Thu, from 11am Fri-Sun, live music 8pm-2am) is famous for its dueling piano acts.

Grab a slice at **New York Pizzeria** (☎702-736-7111; New York–New York; pizza & snacks $4-14; ☉10am-1am Sun-Thu, to 4am Fri & Sat; ♿) or sip North American microbrews at Pour 24 (p32).

Understand
New York in Sin City

With a price tag of $460 million, New York–New York opened in1997. A few years later, after the terrorist attacks of September 11, 2001, spontaneous tributes – predominantly T-shirts from police and fire companies around the nation – started pouring into the Vegas resort. These were displayed for more than a decade, a sort of impromptu monument, in front of New York–New York's Lady Liberty statue.

Vegetarians aren't totally left out, with herb-crusted goat cheese salad, baked brie with oven-roasted tomatoes and fried pickles on the menu.

Zumanity
Billed as 'the sensual side of Cirque du Soleil,' this **human zoo** (📞866-815-4365; www.zumanity.com; tickets $69-105, love seats per couple $250; ⏰7pm & 9:30pm Fri-Tue) amps up the energy, contorted acrobatics and flirtatious eroticism of the troupe's other risk-taking Strip shows. It won't take your breath away, though. So what's the hook? Maybe it's the curvilinear thrust stage, uninhibited costumes or the aphrodisiacal cocktail menu. No guests under 18 years old admitted. Be sure to shop around for tickets as bargains can be found.

Pour 24
Upstairs next to the skybridge entrance, **Pour 24** (📞702-740-6969; ⏰24hr) looks like just any other standard casino bar. The draw is the long list of American craft beers – like Dogfish Head's 60 Minute IPA and Big Sky's Moose Drool – on draft and bottled, or create your own tasting flight.

Gallagher's Steak house
This reproduction of a classy NYC **steakhouse** (📞702-740-6450; mains $28-52; ⏰4-11pm Sun-Thu, to midnight Fri & Sat) – the original Gallagher's dates from 1927 – drums up a serious dinner menu with lobster bisque, wedge salads, dry-aged bone-in sirloin (the house specialty, which you'll see hanging in glass-fronted meat lockers out front) and side dishes like housemade potato chips. The circular bar is an atmospheric spot for a martini with your bros.

Il Fornaio Bakery & Cafe
Take a bite of wood-fired pizza, pasta and salads at this classic NY-style Italian **joint** (📞702-650-6500; www.ilfornaio.com; mains breakfast $9-12, dinner $14-40; ⏰11:30am-11pm Sun-Thu, to midnight Fri & Sat). House specialties include lasagna layered with porcini mushrooms; cannelloni stuffed with rotisserie chicken, organic spinach and smoked mozzarella; and spicy linguine tossed with clams, mussels, prawns and scallops. Gourmet omelets bring out the breakfast crowd.

NEW YORK–NEW YORK

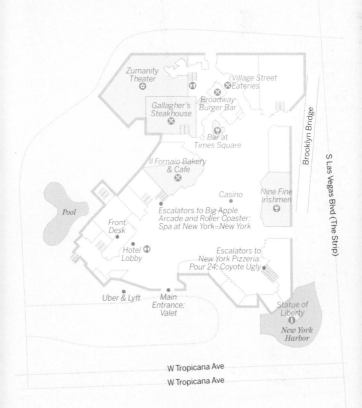

Zumanity Theater

Gallagher's Steakhouse

Village Street Eateries

Broadway Burger Bar

Bar at Times Square

Il Fornaio Bakery & Cafe

Casino

Nine Fine Irishmen

Brooklyn Bridge

S Las Vegas Blvd (The Strip)

Pool

Front Desk

Escalators to Big Apple Arcade and Roller Coaster; Spa at New York–New York

Hotel Lobby

Escalators to New York Pizzeria; Pour 24; Coyote Ugly

Uber & Lyft

Main Entrance; Valet

Statue of Liberty

New York Harbor

W Tropicana Ave

W Tropicana Ave

Top Sights
LINQ Promenade

A mammoth open-air dining, entertainment and retail complex, the $550-million LINQ project has transformed the once-lackluster stretch of the center Strip between the vintage Flamingo and rebranded LINQ casino hotels. Eclectic shops, buzzing bars, trendy restaurants, live-music venues and even a bowling alley line the pedestrian LINQ Promenade. Above it all rises the landmark High Roller observation wheel.

Map p52, C5

www.caesars.com/linq

⊙ 24hr

P ♦

The High Roller and LINQ Promenade

High Roller

The world's largest observation wheel, the **High Roller** (☏702-322-0591; www.caesars.com/linq; adult/child from $22/9, after 5pm $32/19; ⏰11:30am-2am; P🚻; 🚇Flamingo or Harrah's/Linq), towers 550ft above the LINQ's street-level walkways. Each of the 28 air-conditioned passenger cabins is enclosed by handcrafted Italian glass. Outside, 2000 colorful LED lights glow from dusk until dawn. One revolution takes about 30 minutes, and you'll be sharing the ride with a few dozen strangers. Since this is Vegas, the wheelhouse bar sells boozy drinks to take on board.

Polaroid Museum & Fotobar

Print the perfect Vegas selfie on paper, canvas, bamboo or metal at the **Polaroid Fotobar** (☏702-202-2288; ⏰11am-11pm). Then head upstairs to the one-of-a-kind Polaroid Museum (adult/child under 12 years $5/free), which showcases historical artifacts such as large-format Polaroid cameras and also hosts temporary exhibits.

Brooklyn Bowl

Brooklyn Bowl (☏702-862-2695; www.vegas.brooklynbowl.com; 30min lane rental from $25, show tickets $15-70; ⏰5pm-late) is a kind of hybridized high-tech bowling alley/comfort-food-meets-gourmet restaurant and killer concert venue for the kind of indie superbands you'd hear headlining the Coachella or SXSW music festivals.

Virgil's Real BBQ

If you've never tried real-deal Southern cooking, and you're not shy of chunks of mouthwatering smoky meats, baby back ribs, cheesy grits and sugary caramelized sides, you simply must make a beeline for **Virgil's Real BBQ** (☏702-389-7400; www.virgilsbbq.com/locations/las-vegas; mains $10-24; ⏰10am-2am).

☑ Top Tips

▶ From 4pm to 7pm, select pods on the High Roller host the adults-only (21-plus) 'happy half hour' with an open bar (read all-you-can-drink) shared between your fellow riders.

▶ The southwest corner of each High Roller pod affords the best views of the Strip (that's to the right of the door as you enter).

▶ LINQ's shiny new casino, (p54) including its lovingly reinvented O'Sheas pub casino, is a great place for a first flutter.

✖ Take a Break

For quick bites, head to **Jaburrito,** (☏702-901-7375; www.jaburritos.com; LINQ Promenade; items $7-14; ⏰11am-11pm Sun-Thu, to midnight Fri & Sat) where sushi rolls make food love to the humble burrito, or **Gordon Ramsay Fish & Chips** (☏702-322-0529; www.gordonramsayrestaurants.com; LINQ Promenade; mains $9-18; ⏰11am-10pm).

Top Sights
CityCenter

Goodbye kitschy themes and smoky halls – hello sleek lines and fresh air. Traditionally, themed Strip hotels competed to outdo each other, but CityCenter changed the game by refusing to compete at all. This mini-'city' of cutting-edge hotels, restaurants and designer boutiques is a towering luxury playground, whose design smarts and art have transformed the Strip's skyline and cultural landscape.

👁 Map p52, B6

www.citycenter.com

3780 S Las Vegas Blvd

P

Shops at Crystals

The structure of CityCenter's dazzling shopping mall (p71) is an architectural and cultural attraction in its own right. Admire the angular glass canopy jutting onto Las Vegas Blvd, then walk inside to find a three-story 'treehouse' made of smooth, dark wood, as well as a kid-friendly, high-tech art installation composed of neon tube lights and glass-encased funnels of swirling water.

Fine Art Collection

Worth more than $40 million, CityCenter's thought-provoking **fine art collection** (Aria Fine Art Collection; admission free; ⊙24hr; P) is freely displayed throughout the complex's public spaces. You can pick up a self-guided brochure from hotel and shopping mall concierge desks or download a free mobile walking tour app, but the real appeal is stumbling on unexpected works around every corner.

Cosmopolitan

The Strip's hippest casino resort for now, **Cosmo** (☏702-698-7000; www.cosmopolitanlasvegas.com; 3708 S Las Vegas Blvd; ⊙24hr; P) avoids utter pretension, despite the constant wink-wink, arty-retro flourishes such as the Art-o-Mats (vintage cigarette machines hawking original art rather than nicotine), the help-yourself pool tables surrounded by old-school leather armchairs and the larger-than-life red stiletto heel that you can climb into for a tongue-in-cheek Vegas photo op.

Aria

CityCenter's architectural showpiece, **Aria** (☏702-590-7111; www.aria.com; 3730 S Las Vegas Blvd; ⊙24hr; P) centers on a sophisticated casino accented with sleek chrome, polished stone and dark wood. It's a fitting backdrop for visually stunning

☑ Top Tips

▶ Even if you can't afford to stay here, don't be shy! Be sure to have a wander around Cosmopolitan's fabulous lobby and casino floor and take a look at the free Fine Art Collection (p37).

▶ Cosmopolitan has a 'secret' (unlisted) pizza joint that makes delicious pies. You can find the details pretty easily online, but if in doubt, ask the concierge.

✗ Take a Break

For classy small plates, Cosmopolitan's China Poblano (p60), surprisingly, fuses Chinese and Mexican cuisine remarkably well.

Alternatively, stop for a drink at the designer drool-worthy Chandelier Lounge (p68) or Aria's Lobby Bar.

restaurants, many run by top chefs. Energy-efficient design features and eco-conscious amenities come as standard benefits, whether you find them at the East-meets-West spa or inside your own cocoon-like hotel room or suite.

Mandarin Oriental & Vdara

Despite all its frenetic energy, CityCenter also enfolds two hushed oases, the **Mandarin Oriental** (☎702-590-8888; www.mandarinoriental.com; 3752 S Las Vegas Blvd; r/ste from $239/469; ✳🏵🏊) and all-suites **Vdara** (☎702-590-2111; www.vdara.com; 2600 W Harmon Ave; weekday/weekend ste from $129/189; P🅿✳@🏵🏊🐾) hotels, where you can get away from the ding-ding-ding of the slot machines. Even if you're not staying overnight, ride the elevator to the Mandarin Oriental's 23rd-floor 'sky lobby' to take in nighttime views of the Strip's neon lights while you sip champagne cocktails.

Twist by Pierre Gagnaire

If romantic **Twist's** (☎702-590-8888; Mandarin Oriental; mains $45-95, tasting menus $95-295; ⏰6-10pm Tue-Thu, to 10:30pm Fri & Sat) sparkling nighttime Strip views don't make you gasp, the modern French cuisine by this three-star Michelin chef just might. Seasonal tasting menus at this Mandarin Oriental outpost may include squid-ink gnocchetti topped with carrot gelée or langoustine with grapefruit fondue, finished off with bubble-gum ice cream with marshmallow and green-tea crumbles. Reservations essential; dress code is business casual.

Todd English P.U.B.

Twice-daily happy hours (3pm to 6pm, and 10pm until midnight) with half-price pints and cheap wings, oysters and sliders keep bar stools filled at this cozy brick-walled **pub** (☎702-489-8080; www.cheftoddenglish.com; Shops at Crystals; ⏰11am-2am Mon-Fri, from 9:30am Sat & Sun) with an outdoor patio. The kitchen closes at 11:30pm daily.

CITYCENTER

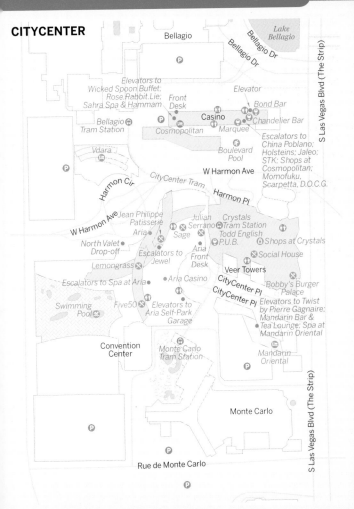

Bellagio

Lake Bellagio

Bellagio Dr

Bellagio Dr

S Las Vegas Blvd (The Strip)

Elevators to
Wicked Spoon Buffet;
Rose.Rabbit.Lie;
Sahra Spa & Hammam

Front
Desk

Elevator

Bond Bar

Chandelier Bar

Casino

Marquee

Cosmopolitan

Bellagio
Tram Station

Vdara

Boulevard
Pool

W Harmon Ave

Escalators to
China Poblano;
Holsteins; Jaleo;
STK; Shops at
Cosmopolitan;
Momofuku,
Scarpetta, D.O.C.G.

Harmon Cir

CityCenter Tram

Harmon Pl

W Harmon Ave

Jean Philippe
Patisserie

Julian
Serrano

Crystals
Tram Station
Todd English
P.U.B.

Shops at Crystals

Aria

Sage

North Valet
Drop-off

Escalators to
Jewel

Aria
Front
Desk

Social House

Lemongrass

Veer Towers

Escalators to Spa at Aria

Aria Casino

CityCenter Pl

Bobby's Burger
Palace

Swimming
Pool

Five50

Elevators to
Aria Self-Park
Garage

CityCenter Pl

Elevators to Twist
by Pierre Gagnaire;
Mandarin Bar &
Tea Lounge; Spa at
Mandarin Oriental

Convention
Center

Monte Carlo
Tram Station

Mandarin
Oriental

Monte Carlo

S Las Vegas Blvd (The Strip)

Rue de Monte Carlo

Top Sights
Paris Las Vegas

Paris Las Vegas aims to emulate the essence of the grand dame by recreating her most famous landmarks, including the Eiffel Tower, Arc de Triomphe and Maritime Fountain from the Place de la Concorde. Somehow, here on the Las Vegas Strip, it succeeds in evoking a sense of the City of Light – right down to the accordion players.

◉ Map p52, C5

☏ 877-603-4386

www.parislasvegas.com

3655 S Las Vegas Blvd

🕑 24hr

P

Eiffel Tower Experience

Families and lovers flock to Vegas' **Eiffel Tower Experience** (📞888-727-4758; www.caesars.com; adult/child 12yr & under/family $19/14/49, after 7:15pm $22/17/67; ⏰9:30am-12:30am Mon-Fri, to 1am Sat & Sun, weather permitting; 🅿️🚹), lining up for grated views from a windblown observation deck. It's cheaper to take a ride on the tower's elevators during the day, but nighttime panoramas of the Strip, when casino neons blink and flicker and the Bellagio's dancing fountains are illuminated, are worth the marginally extra expense.

Eiffel Tower Restaurant

With all of Vegas' high-end and celebrity dining to choose from, it might feel a bit cheesy to dine at a theme-park-ish replica of the planet's ultimate symbol of romance, but don't be too quick to judge: the ruse is convincing. At this haute **restaurant** (📞702-948-6937; www.eiffeltowerrestaurant.com; mains lunch $14-32, dinner $32-89, tasting menu without/with wine pairings $125/205; ⏰11:30am-10pm Mon-Fri, 11am-11pm Sat & Sun) midway up its namesake tower, the Francophile wine list is vast, the chocolate soufflé is unforgettable, and views of the Strip and Bellagio's fountains are breathtaking. Lunch is your best bet, but it's more popular to come at sunset. Reservations essential.

Beer Park

Occupying a prime spot beneath Paris' Eiffel Tower, **Beer Park (by Budweiser)** (📞702-444-4500; www.beerpark.com; ⏰11am-2am Mon-Fri, from 9am Sat & Sun) is an open-air beer garden overlooking the Fountains of Bellagio. With tap varieties from around the world and a friendly, easy vibe, it's a cinch to meet other travelers or lovers of the amber liquid. But be warned: it's also an easy spot to get lazy!

☑ Top Tips

▶ If you don't have the cash to enjoy dining at the Eiffel Tower, or even riding to the observation deck, one of the best free hangs for watching Bellagio's dancing fountains is Beer Park. Do the right thing, though, and buy one beer, at least.

▶ The best spots for photographing the Eiffel Tower are found by making like a tree and cozy-ing up to the trunks across the Strip, adjacent to Bellagio's Lake Como.

✖ Take a Break

You can't go past Beer Park for a casual, relaxed place to rest your weary legs, take in the surroundings and enjoy a cold beer or light meal.

If you just need a quick, cheap feed (sans views), head around the corner for Cali-Japanese ramen at Ramen-ya Katana (p58).

Spa by Mandara

At this full-service salon and **spa** (☎702-946-4366; www.mandaraspa.com; fitness center day pass nonguests $25; ⊙7am-7pm, fitness center from 6am), which mixes Balinese and European influences, the most luxurious treatment rooms have handcrafted tropical hardwood, Matisse-styled artworks and silk carpets. Couples can opt for the 'Paris for Lovers' treatment package, including a whirlpool tub made for two. Complimentary fitness center access comes with spa treatments over $50.

Le Cabaret

In a city where tickets to a show can cost a small fortune, it's nice to know that some of the good things in life are still free. Just off Paris Las Vegas' casino floor, the intimate **Le Cabaret** (☎702-946-7000; www.caesars.com; ⊙9pm-1am Sun-Thu, to 2am Fri & Sat) hosts a nightly schedule of live jazz where sultry lounge singers will have you almost believing you've stepped into a bar in Saint-Germain.

Chateau Nightclub & Gardens

Hip-hop prevails at this rooftop **venue** (☎702-776-7770; www.chateaunights.com; ⊙10pm-4am Wed, Fri & Sat) landscaped to look like Parisian gardens. Views over the Strip are divine from tiered outdoor terraces while, back inside, go-go dancers do their thing above a small dancefloor, which can be half empty even on weekends. Sometimes on summer days, the lounge space on the open-air deck doubles as a beer garden.

Napoleon's Dueling Pianos

At this **bar** (☎702-7000; www.caesars.com; ⊙bar 6pm-2am), you get whisked off to the never-never land of 19th-century France, with a mosaic floor and overstuffed sofas as luxurious as the menu of 100 types of bubbly, including vintage Dom Pérignon for big spenders. Dueling pianos draw a crowd; there's no cover charge, but expect a two-drink minimum.

Gordon Ramsay Steak

Carnivores, leave Paris behind and stroll through a miniaturized Chunnel into British chef Gordon Ramsay's **steakhouse** (☎877-346-4642; www.gordon-ramsayrestaurants.com; mains $32-105, tasting menu without/with wine pairings $145/220; ⊙4:30-10:30pm daily, bar to midnight Fri & Sat). Ribboned in red and domed by a jaunty Union Jack, this is one of the top tables in town. Fish, chops and beef Wellington round out a menu of Himalayan-salt-room-aged steaks. No reservation? Sit at the bar.

Mon Ami Gabi

Think très charming Champs-Élysées **bistro** (☎702-944-4224; www.monamigabi.com; mains $12-40; ⊙7am-11pm). Breezy patio tables in the shadow of the Eiffel Tower are *parfait* for alfresco dining and watching the Fountains of Bellagio. Though spotty service is far from *magnifique,* it's got classic steak frites and mussels, crepes, quiches and salads, plus a respectable wine list and a special gluten-free menu. Reservations recommended for indoor seating; the patio is first-come, first-served.

PARIS LAS VEGAS

Paris Ballroom

Elevators to Self-Parking Garage

Napoleon's Dueling Pianos

Convention Center

Bally's/Paris Las Vegas Monorail Station

Le Boulevard

Elevators to Spa By Mandara; Swimming Pool

Le Village Buffet

La Creperie

Anthony Cools

Paris Dr

Café Belle Madeleine

Front Desk; Hotel Lobby

Gordon Ramsey Steak

Paris Las Vegas Casino

Main Entrance

Arc de Triomphe

Bridge to Eiffel Tower Experience

Le Cabaret

Valet

Elevators to Eiffel Tower Restaurant

Mon Ami Gabi

Eiffel Tower Restaurant

Chateau Nightclub & Gardens

Eiffel Tower Experience

Beer Park (by Budweiser)

S Las Vegas Blvd (The Strip)

Top Sights
Venetian & Palazzo

Inspired by the splendor of Italy's most romantic city, the Venetian (opened in 1999) boasts reproductions of Venetian landmarks. Its grandiose sequel resort, the adjacent Palazzo, threw open its doors to a sophisticated crowd in 2008. You can walk from Vegas' Venice to its offshore island in just a few minutes, but gondoliers are available to complete the experience.

👁 Map p52, C4

Venetian 📞 702-414-1000;
Palazzo 📞 702-607-7777

www.venetian.com;
www.palazzo.com

3325-55 S Las Vegas Blvd

🕑 24hr

Ⓟ

Gondola ride

Slice of Italy

Even if you've had the good fortune to stroll the cobblestones and navigate the romantic canals of the world-famous Italian port city, you won't want to miss the Vegas version: in a city filled with spectacles, the Venetian is one of the most magnificent. Graceful bridges, flowing canals and vibrant piazzas faithfully imitate the Venetian spirit.

Architecture

In the ongoing contest for Vegas' best copycat architecture, the Venetian wins the prize for elegant design, just edging ahead of Bellagio, its Italianate rival down the Strip. View the stunning exterior while approaching it over a pedestrian skybridge. Notice the scaled-down replicas of the **Palazzo Ducale**, the towering **Campanile** (bell tower), the mini **Rialto Bridge** (anachronistically equipped with escalators) and a crowded cobblestone **piazza** where tourists gaze down at couples canoodling in gondolas steered by striped-shirted boaters. Inside the Grand Canal Shoppes (p46), colorfully dressed minstrels and operatic sopranos stroll past patrons sipping wine at faux-outdoor cafes in a miniaturized **Piazza San Marco**.

Gondola Ride

If you can't make it to Venice to experience the real thing, a **gondola ride** (📞 702-414-4300; www.venetian.com/resort/attractions/gondola-rides.html; Venetian; shared ride per person $29, child under 3yr free, private 2-passenger ride $116; ⏰ indoor 10am-11pm Sun-Thu, to midnight Fri & Sat, outdoor rides 11am-10pm, weather permitting; 👪) in Vegas is a touristy activity that nonetheless holds allure for visitors from all over the world. Choose between a moonlit outdoor cruise in the resort's miniature lake facing the Strip or float through winding indoor canals

☑ **Top Tips**

▶ Rooms at Palazzo and Venetian are similar in size, design and price, but the Palazzo is almost a decade younger than its older sister, the Venetian.

▶ The gaming floors, Grand Canal Shoppes and hotel wings of the Palazzo and Venetian are all joined by indoor and outdoor walkways, but taking a gondola ride is a fun (albeit expensive) way to get an overview of Vegas' little slice of Italy.

✖ **Take a Break**

For a happening vibe and the fusion of Latin and Japanese cuisine, pop into **Sushisamba** (📞 702-607-0700; www.sushisamba.com; Grand Canal Shoppes at the Palazzo; shared plates $3-28, mains $26-57; ⏰ 11:30am-1am Sun-Wed, to 2am Thu-Sat).

If alcohol is on your mind, you can't go past the ineffably stylish and recently renovated **Dorsey** (📞 702-414-1945; www.venetian.com; Venetian; ⏰ 2pm-4am).

past shoppers and diners. Buy tickets inside the Grand Canal Shoppes at the Venetian.

Grand Canal Shoppes

Don't be surprised if you come across Hollywood celebrities wandering about the high-design **Grand Canal Shoppes at the Palazzo** (☎702-414-4525; www.grandcanalshoppes.com; 3377 S Las Vegas Blvd, Palazzo; ⏰10am-11pm Sun-Thu, to midnight Fri & Sat), anchored by the three-story Barneys New York. It's joined to the **Grand Canal Shoppes at the Venetian** (☎702-414-4525; www.grandcanalshoppes.com; 3377 S Las Vegas Blvd, Venetian; ⏰10am-11pm Sun-Thu, to midnight Fri & Sat), where wandering painted minstrels, jugglers and laughable living statues perform in Piazza San Marco as gondolas drift by and mezzo-sopranos serenade shoppers. In this airy Italianate mall adorned with frescoes and cobblestone walkways, you'll find an additional 85 luxury boutiques.

Canyon Ranch SpaClub

The modern **Canyon Ranch SpaClub** (☎877-220-2688; www.canyonranch.com/las-vegas; 3355 S Las Vegas Blvd #1159, Grand Canal Shoppes; ⏰spa 6am-8pm, salon 9am-7pm), a health-minded spa from Arizona, couldn't feel further from the alleys and canals of Venice, but, nonetheless, here it is. With a focus on well-being and offering more than 100 spa and salon services and fitness activities, it specializes in massage and couples' side-by-side therapies. On the spa's hydrotherapy circuit, you can move lazily from a herbal laconium to the salt grotto to a meditative wave room. The spa cafe serves light cuisine and fresh fruit smoothies.

Palazzo: Refined Luxury

The sophisticated Palazzo (p44) lacks a theme, following the Strip's trend toward ever more refined luxury. Forget fun-loving circus acts and exploding volcanoes: the Palazzo is a luxe casino resort best known for its haute cuisine, cool pool club and high-end shopping. Enormous suites come with sunken living rooms and Roman tubs, while Prestige Suites enjoy VIP check-in with complimentary champagne.

Bouchon

Napa Valley wunderkind Thomas Keller's rendition of a Lyonnaise bistro, **Bouchon** (☎702-414-6200; www.thomaskeller.com/bouchonlasvegas; Venetian; mains breakfast & brunch $12-26, dinner $19-51; ⏰7am-1pm & 5-10pm Mon-Fri, 7am-2pm & 5-10pm Sat & Sun; P☑) features a seasonal menu of French classics. The poolside setting complements the oyster bar (open 3pm to 10pm daily) and an extensive raw seafood selection. Decadent breakfasts and brunches, imported cheeses, caviar, foie gras and a superb French and Californian wine list all make appearances. Reservations recommended.

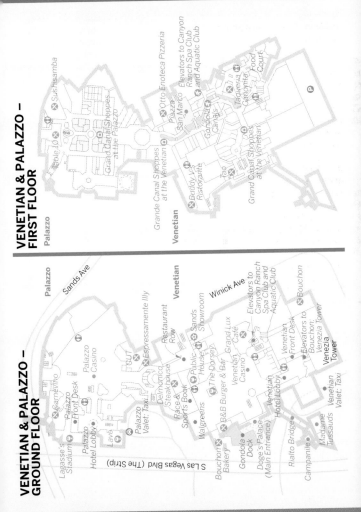

VENETIAN & PALAZZO –
FIRST FLOOR

Palazzo

Sushisamba

Grand Canal Shoppes at the Palazzo

Table 10

Otto Enoteca Pizzeria

Elevators to Canyon Ranch Spa Club and Aquatic Club

San Marco

Food Court

Taqueria Canonita

Grande Canal Shoppes at the Venetian

Gondola Canals

Buddy V Ristorante

Tao

Grand Canal Shoppes at the Venetian

Venetian

VENETIAN & PALAZZO –
GROUND FLOOR

Palazzo

Sands Ave

Venetian

Winick Ave

Lagasse's Stadium

Carnevino

Palazzo Front Desk

Palazzo Casino

Espressamente Illy

TOUT

Restaurant Row

Sands Showroom

Elevators to Canyon Ranch Spa Club and Aquatic Club

Palazzo Hotel Lobby

Lavo

Delmonico Steakhouse

Public House

Grand Lux Café

Bouchon

Race & Sports Book

The Dorsey

Venetian Front Desk

Palazzo Valet: Taxi

Walgreens

B&B Burger & Bar

Venetian Casino

Elevators to Bouchon: Venezia Tower

S Las Vegas Blvd (The Strip)

Bouchon Bakery

Gondola Dock

Doge's Palace (Main Entrance)

Venetian Hotel Lobby

Venetian Valet: Taxi

Rialto Bridge

Madame Tussauds

Campanile

Top Sights
Wynn & Encore

Instead of featuring an exploding volcano or an Eiffel Tower to lure people, casino impresario Steve Wynn's curvaceous, copper-toned twins Wynn (opened in 2005) and Encore (2008) are all about exclusivity. Elements of the casino mogul's former projects peek through: Wynn sports the style of Bellagio but is more vibrant, while Encore feels like a slice of the French Riviera.

◉ Map p52, C4

☏ 702-770-7000

www.wynnlasvegas.com

3131 S Las Vegas Blvd

🕐 24hr

🅿

Wynn

Steve Wynn's signature casino hotel (literally – his name is written in script across the top of the Wynn) exudes secrecy: the entrance is obscured from the Strip by an artificial mountain of greenery, which rises seven stories tall in places. Inside, the resort comes alive with vibrant colors, inlaid flower mosaics, natural-light windows, lush foliage and tumbling waterfalls.

Encore

Wynn's penmanship also labels the adjacent Encore resort, where jeweled peacocks grace the elegant baccarat room and high rollers throw back martinis in cushy casino bars. Sunning yourself at fashionable Encore Beach Club (p67) on blazing hot summer days, you might feel like you're an extra in a hip-hop superstar's music video. Back inside the resort, glam XS (p66) and Surrender (p66) nightclubs host world-renowned DJs and musicians. The extravagant Spa at Encore (p50) is the Strip's best for beautifying or, after a big night, detoxifying.

Le Rêve the Dream

Created by ex–Cirque du Soleil director Franco Dragone, the dreamy, fanciful and occasionally nightmarish series of vignettes that make up **Le Rêve the Dream** (☑ 702-770-9966; http://boxoffice. wynnlasvegas.com; Wynn; tickets $105-205; ⊙7pm & 9:30pm Fri-Tue) cost Steve Wynn many millions – and made him many more. Underwater acrobatic feats by scuba-certified performers are the centerpiece of this intimate 'aqua-in-the-round' theater, which holds a 1-million-gallon swimming pool. Critics call it a less-inspiring version of Cirque's O, while devoted fans find the romantic underwater tango, thrilling high dives and visually spectacular adventures to be superior.

☑ Top Tips

▶ As exclusive as Wynn and Encore are, and as stylish as they appear to be, they're both still casinos filled with gaming tables, restaurants and boutiques designed to take your money. Don't be shy: even if you're not a hotel guest, your presence is desired.

▶ While the 'twins' look the same from the outside, each has a very different vibe. Of Vegas' return high rollers, Wynn has its staunch supporters, while newer Encore seems to attract a slightly younger, though equally cashed-up crowd, never more evident than at its drool-worthy Beach Club.

✗ Take a Break

Pop into recently refurbished Parasol Up & Parasol Down (p50) to rest your legs and sip on classy cocktails.

The cheapest seats are in the 'splash zone,' while VIP packages come with champagne and chocolate-covered strawberries.

Intrigue Nightclub

Since its much anticipated opening in spring 2017, Wynn's (and Vegas') newest, state-of-the-art nightclub, **Intrigue** (📞702-770-7300; www.intriguevegas.com; Wynn; 🕐10pm-4am Thu-Sat), has been turning heads the length of the Strip with its 14,000ft of after-dark dreams come true: think Studio 54 meets the new millennium. It's chic, sleek and if you don't dress to dazzle you won't even get close to the queue.

Parasol Up & Parasol Down

Stepping into the whimsical jewel-hued **Parasol Up** (📞702-770-3392; www.wynnlasvegas.com; Wynn; 🕐11am-3am Sun-Thu, to 4am Fri & Sat, Parasol Down 11am-2am; 🚇Deuce) feels something like walking into a glamorous version of *Alice in Wonderland*, complete with bright, almost psychedelic flowers. Cozy up on a plush ruby-red loveseat and gaze out at the glassy Lake of Dreams. Down the fairy-tale-like curved escalator, **Parasol Down's** seasonal outdoor patio is the perfect spot for cucumber and ginger-infused martinis.

Costa di Mare

Even in Vegas it doesn't get much posher than **Costa di Mare** (📞702-770-3305; www.wynnlasvegas.com; Wynn; mains $30-60, tasting menus $150-180; 🕐5:30-10pm; 🅿❄🍷), where you can book a private cabana beside Wynn's Lake of Dreams and dine on fresh Mediterranean blue rock lobster under a fluttering white canopy. The upscale Italian-style seafood restaurant has a short, highly specialized menu – the whole fish served are indigenous to Italy, and simply prepared. Reservations essential.

Spa at Encore

Newer than the spa at Wynn, Encore's luxurious **spa** (📞702-770-3900; Encore; spa & fitness center day pass $40; 🕐7am-8pm) is splurge-worthy. Stroll down exotic, tranquil passageways lined with flickering Middle Eastern lamps and golden Buddha statues, then sink into hot or cold plunge pools under glowing Swarovski crystal chandeliers, or recline on a heated chaise longue before trying a Thai oil fusion massage or the Moroccan mud wrap. The spa and fitness center entry fee is waived with a treatment of $75 or more.

SW Steakhouse

Bearing Steve Wynn's own initials, **SW Steakhouse** (📞702-770-3325; www.wynnlasvegas.com; Wynn; mains $35-65; 🕐5:30-10pm; ❄) is not just any casino steakhouse: it's perched on the shore of the petite Lake of Dreams. A well-executed classic steakhouse menu hits all the right notes, from oysters on the half shell to chili-rubbed rib-eye steak and black-truffle creamed corn. Reservations are essential, especially for the coveted tables on the open-air terrace.

WYNN & ENCORE

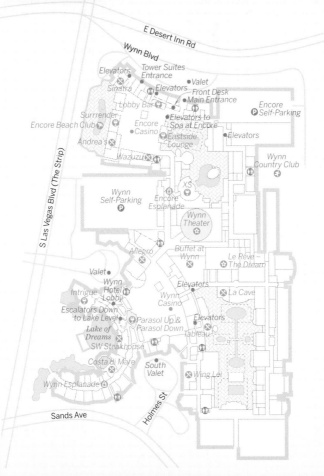

E Desert Inn Rd

Wynn Blvd

Elevators
Tower Suites Entrance
•Valet
Sinatra
Elevators
Front Desk
•Main Entrance
Lobby Bar
Encore
P Self-Parking
Surrender
Elevators to
Spa at Encore
Encore Beach Club
Encore
•Casino
Elevators
Andrea's
Eastside
Lounge
Wazuzu
Wynn
Country Club

S Las Vegas Blvd (The Strip)

XS

Wynn
Self-Parking
P
Encore
Esplanade
Wynn
Theater

Allegro
Buffet at
Wynn
Le Rêve –
The Dream
La Cave

Valet•
Wynn
Hotel
Lobby
Intrigue
Escalators Down
to Lake Level
Elevators
Wynn
Casino
Parasol Up &
Parasol Down
Elevators
Tableau
Lake of
Dreams
SW Steakhouse

Costa di Mare
Wing Lei
Wynn Esplanade
South
Valet

Sands Ave

Holmes St

Canosa Ave

State St

Wynn Golf
and Country
Club

Joe W Brown Dr

Sierra Vista Dr

Swenson St

Stratosphere
Thrill Rides

S 6th St

Karen Ave

Westgate
Las Vegas

Las Vegas
Convention
Center

E Desert Inn Rd

Elm Dr

E Twain Ave

E Sahara Ave

Paradise Rd

Paradise Rd

14 🏠 SLS

⊗23 45 🏠

⊗ ⊗
21

Cleveland Ave

2 🏠 6

Stratosphere

Las Vegas
Convention &
Visitors Authority

Riviera Blvd

S Las Vegas Blvd (The Strip)

Convention Center Dr

Wynn
Golf Club

Sands Ave

Highland Ave

Western Ave

⊗19

⊗15

33 32

25 ⊗17

35 ⊗

Wynn & Encore
Casinos

Venetian

S Rancho Dr

Circus Circus

Adventuredome

9 ⊗

7

Circus Circus

Desert Inn Rd Super-Arterial

40 🏠

Palazzo

Treasure
Island

11

Mirage

Mirage

W Sahara Ave

Sammy Davis Jr Dr

Highland Dr

Westwood Dr

Rancho Dr

Merritt Ave

Kings Ave

Wilmington Way

Milo Way

Meade Ave

Sirius Ave

Capella Ave

W Desert Inn Rd

S Spring Mountain Rd

W Spring Mountain Rd

W Twain Ave

El Conlon Ave

S Valley View Blvd

For reviews see

◎	Top Sights	p22
⊙	Sights	p54
⊗	Eating	p57
🍷	Drinking	p64
🎭	Entertainment	p68
🛍	Shopping	p71

Flamingo Wash

University of Nevada, Las Vegas (UNLV)

Swenson St

Tropicana Wash

E Flamingo Rd

Paradise Rd

Paradise Rd

Rent A Car Rd

1 km

0.5 miles

E Flamingo Rd

Naples Dr

E Tropicana Ave

E Harmon Ave

Harrah's/The LINQ

LINQ Casino

Lana Ave

McCarran International Airport

N

LINQ Promenade

Flamingo/Caesars Palace

Bally's/Paris Las Vegas

Koval La

Flamingo Wildlife Habitat

MGM Grand

13

34

Paris Las Vegas

16

22

Audrie St

E Reno Ave

Mandalay Bay Rd

THE STRIP

44

27

43

MGM Grand

Haven St

CITYCENTER

3

Giles St

Diablo Dr

S Las Vegas Blvd (The Strip)

39

38

36

Caesars Palace & Spa

5

42

30

Qua Baths & Spa

Bellagio

29

28

41

31

CityCenter

Monte Carlo

37

Excalibur

Luxor

10

8

Luxor

Mandalay Bay

24

18

26 20

Bellagio

CityCenter

New York–New York

Mandalay Bay

Dean Martin Dr

Aldebaran Ave

W Harmon Ave

Tompkins Ave

W Tropicana Ave

Ali Baba La

Polaris Ave

Polaris Ave

Nevso Dr

S Valley View Blvd

Procyon Ave

S Valley View Blvd

W Hacienda Ave

Viking Rd

W Flamingo Rd

Wynn Rd

Sights

LINQ Casino
CASINO

1 ⊙ Map p52, C5

With a fresh, young and funky vibe, one of Vegas' newest casinos benefits from also being one of its smallest with just over 60 tables and around 750 slot machines. There's an airy, spacious feel to the place, tables feature high-backed, ruby-red, patent-vinyl chairs, and when you need to escape, the fun and frivolity of LINQ Promenade (p34) is just outside the door. (✆800-634-6441; www.caesars.com/linq; 3535 S Las Vegas Blvd; ⊙24hr; P)

Stratosphere
CASINO

2 ⊙ Map p52, D1

Vegas has many buildings over 20 stories tall, but only Stratosphere exceeds 100 and boasts the nation's highest thrill rides. Atop the 1149ft-high tapered tripod tower, vertiginous indoor and outdoor viewing decks afford Vegas' best 360-degree panoramas. There you'll also find Top of the World (p62), a revolving restaurant, and the jazzy 107 SkyLounge (p66) cocktail bar. To get to the top of Vegas' lucky landmark, ride one of America's fastest elevators, lifting you 108 floors in a mere 37 ear-popping seconds. (✆702-380-7777; www.stratospherehotel.com; 2000 S Las Vegas Blvd; tower entry adult/child $20/10, all-day pass incl unlimited thrill rides $40; ⊙casino 24hr, tower & thrill rides 10am-1am Sun-Thu, to 2am Fri & Sat, weather permitting; P👪)

MGM Grand
CASINO

3 ⊙ Map p52, C7

Owned by the eponymous Hollywood studio, the Grand liberally borrows Hollywood themes. Flashing LED screens and computerized fountains add extra theatrics to the 100,000lb, 45ft-tall bronze lion statue at the casino's entrance. Inside the labyrinthine casino bedecked with giant screens, you can get table-side massages or take free Texas hold'em lessons in the poker room. Top billing attractions include Hakkasan (p64) nightclub, one-time center of the electronic dance-music universe, Cirque du Soleil's martial-arts-inspired **Kà** (✆702-531-3826; www.cirquedusoleil.com; adult $69-150, child 5-12yr $35-75; ⊙7pm & 9:30pm Sat-Wed; 👪) and the massive **MGM Grand Garden Arena** (✆877-880-0880; www.mgmgrand.com/entertainment; ticket prices vary; ⊙box office 9am-8:30pm 3799 S Las Vegas Blvd; ⊙24hr; P👪)

Caesars Palace
CASINO

4 ⊙ Map p52, B5

Caesars Palace claims that its smartly renovated casino floor has more million-dollar slots than anywhere in the world, but its claims to fame are far more numerous than that. Entertainment's heavyweights Celine Dion and Elton John 'own' its custom-built Colosseum (p70) theater, fashionistas saunter around the Shops at Forum (p72), while Caesars group hotel guests quaff cocktails in the **Garden of the Gods Pool Oasis**. By night,

JASON PATRICK ROSS/SHUTTERSTOCK ©

The Strip

megaclub Omnia (p65) is the *only* place to get off your face this side of Ibiza. (☎866-227-5938; www.caesarspalace. com; 3570 S Las Vegas Blvd; ☺24hr; P)

Qua Baths & Spa SPA

5 ◉ Map p52, C5

Qua evokes the ancient Roman rituals of indulgent bathing. Try a signature 'bath liqueur,' a personalized potion of herbs and oils poured into your own private tub. The women's side includes a tea lounge, a herbal steam room and an Arctic ice room where artificial snow falls. On the men's side, there's a barber spa and big-screen sports TVs. (☎866-782-0655; Caesars Palace; fitness center day pass $25, incl spa facilities $50; ☺6am-8pm)

Stratosphere Thrill Rides AMUSEMENT PARK

6 ◉ Map p52, D1

The world's highest thrill rides await, a whopping 110 stories above the Strip. Big Shot straps riders into completely exposed seats that zip up the tower's pinnacle, while Insanity spins riders out over the tower's edge. X-Scream leaves you hanging 27ft over the edge, 866ft above ground. For a real adrenaline rush, save your dough for **SkyJump**. (☎702-383-5210; www.stratospherehotel. com/Attractions/Thrill-Rides; Stratosphere; elevator adult $20, incl 3 thrill rides $35, all-day pass $40; ☺10am-1am Sun-Thu, to 2am Fri & Sat; ☐Sahara)

Local Life

Public Oasis

For some reason in such a sunshine-filled place, it took 60 years for an outdoor park to be built on the Las Vegas Strip. The new-in-2016 **Park** (📞702-693-7275; www.theparkvegas.com/en.html; 3782 S Las Vegas Blvd; 🚻) is a public place with plenty of visual appeal; waterworks and fountains line tree-shaded pathways festooned with restaurants, such as the eatery Bruxie where Belgian waffles are united with fried chicken. Rare for the Strip, it's a place that's suitable for children as well as adults.

Adventuredome AMUSEMENT PARK

7 ◉ Map p52, C2

Enclosed by over 8000 pink-glass panes, Circus Circus' indoor amusement park is packed with thrills. Must-rides include the double-loop, double-corkscrew Canyon Blaster and the gravity-defying El Loco that packs a whopping -1.5 Gs of vertical acceleration. Older kids get a rock-climbing wall, bungee-jumping area, mini golf and 4D special-effect 'ridefilms.' Clowns perform free shows throughout the day. (📞702-794-3939; www.adventuredome.com; Circus Circus; day pass over/under 48in tall $32/18; ⏰10am-6pm daily, later on weekends & May-Sep; 🚻)

Welcome to Las Vegas Sign LANDMARK

8 ◉ Map p52, C8

In a city famous for neon signs, one reigns supreme: the 'Welcome to Fabulous Las Vegas Nevada' sign, facing north and straddling Las Vegas Blvd just south of Mandalay Bay (p26), the unofficial beginning of the Strip. Designed by Betty Willis at the end of the 'Fabulous Fifties,' this Googie-style sign is a classic photo op and a reminder of Vegas' past. Only southbound traffic can enter the parking lot, greeted by its flip-side reminder to 'Drive Carefully' and 'Come Back Soon.' (5200 S Las Vegas Blvd; admission free; ⏰24hr; 🚻)

Circus Circus CASINO

9 ◉ Map p52, C2

If you belong to that special (in a nice way) bunch of people who are terrified by clowns, do not under any circumstances venture near this somewhat bedraggled part of the north Strip: if the enormous clown sign isn't impossible to handle, you'll lose it at the clown-shaped marquee (there *are* real-life clowns inside). Although this ole circus with its big-top casino is as cheesy as it looks, it can also be lots of fun, especially if you have kids. (📞702-734-0410; www.circuscircus.com; 2880 S Las Vegas Blvd; ⏰24hr; 🅿 🚻)

Luxor CASINO

10 ⊚ Map p52, B8

Named after Egypt's splendid ancient city on the east bank of the Nile, the landmark Luxor once had the biggest wow factor on the south Strip. While the theme easily could have produced a pyramid of gaudiness, instead it resulted in a relatively refined shrine to Egyptian art, architecture and antiquities. Luxor's casino floor has a slightly frenetic feel and confusing layout, with a few thousand slots, more than 100 gaming tables, and a race and sports book. (☎702-262-4000; www.luxor. com; 3900 S Las Vegas Blvd; ◷24hr; Ⓟ)

Mirage CASINO

11 ⊚ Map p52, B4

Having somewhat shaken its historically tropical theme, the Mirage retains its huge rainforest atrium of lush, tropical foliage and has updated the 20,000-gallon saltwater aquarium in the lobby. Its renovated casino floor features an updated sports book, huge new **Center Bar**, more than 100 tables and over 2000 slots, and a revamped poker room offering daily tournaments and complimentary lessons. (☎702-791-7111; www.mirage.com; 3400 S Las Vegas Blvd; ◷24hr; Ⓟ)

Mirage Volcano LANDMARK

12 ⊚ Map p52, C4

When the Mirage's trademark artificial volcano erupts with a roar out of a 3-acre lagoon, it inevitably brings traffic on the Strip to a screeching halt. Be on the lookout for wisps of smoke escaping from the top, signaling that the fiery Polynesian-style inferno, with a soundtrack by a Grateful Dead drummer and an Indian tabla musician, is about to begin. (☎800-374-9000; www. mirage.com; Mirage; admission free; ◷shows 8pm & 9pm daily, also 10pm Fri & Sat)

Flamingo Wildlife Habitat GARDENS

13 ⊚ Map p52, C5

Slip away from the madness inside the **Flamingo's** (☎702-733-3111; www. flamingolasvegas.com; 3555 S Las Vegas Blvd; ◷24hr; Ⓟ) wildlife habitat, out back behind the casino. Over a dozen acres of pools, gardens, waterfalls and waterways are filled with swans, exotic birds and ornamental koi (carp). Here, Chilean flamingos and African penguins wander around, and palm trees and jungle plants flourish in the middle of the desert. (☎702-733-3349; Flamingo; admission free; ◷8am-dusk, pelican feedings 8:30am & 2pm; Ⓟ ⓖ)

Eating

Umami Burger BURGERS $

14 ✗ Map p52, D2

The burgers on offer at SLS Hotel and Casino are some of the best on the Strip, with its outdoor beer garden, extensive craft beer selection and juicy boutique burgers made by the chain that won *GQ* magazine's prestigious 'burger of the year' crown. (📞702-761-7614; www.slslasvegas.com/dining/umami-burger; SLS, 2535 S Las Vegas Blvd; burgers $12-15; ⏱11am-10pm; 🅿)

Tacos El Gordo   MEXICAN $

15 🍴 Map p52, C3

This Tijuana-style taco shop from SoCal is just the ticket when it's way late, you've got almost no money left and you're desperately craving *carne asada* (beef) or *adobada* (chile-marinated pork) tacos in hot, hand-made tortillas. Adventurous eaters order the authentic *sesos* (beef brains), *cabeza* (roasted cow's head) or tripe (intestines) variations. (📞702-251-8226; www.tacoselgordobc.com; 3049 S Las Vegas Blvd; small plates $3-12; ⏱10am-2am Sun-Thu, to 4am Fri & Sat; 🅿🖊🚻; 🚌Deuce, SDX)

Ramen-ya Katana   RAMEN $

16 🍴 Map p52, C5

Granted, purists who follow the Japanese religion of ramen might get picky, but we won't. In a sea of complicated, overpriced and prohibitive dining, Katana offers humble bowls of hot broth swimming with hearty noodles at *almost* normal prices, on the center Strip. In true San Franciscan fashion, they've even thrown sushi burritos on the menu. Winning! (📞702-586-6889; www.ramen-katanaya.com; 3615 S Las Vegas Blvd, Grand Bazaar Shops; meals $9-14; ⏱9:30am-1am; ❄)

La Cave   MEDITERRANEAN $$

17 🍴 Map p52, C4

Flavorful seasonal tapas, brick-oven-fired flatbreads and Mediterranean-inspired plates, all meant for sharing, are the ticket at this laid-back hideaway. With romantic candlelight, Spanish-style archways and a pool-view patio, La Cave is a secluded spot for a dinner date or a few glasses of tempranillo with an artisanal cheese or charcuterie board. (📞702-770-7375; www.wynnlasvegas.com; Wynn; shared plates $9-22; ⏱11:30am-10pm Mon-Thu, to 11pm Fri & Sat, 10:30am-2:30pm & 4-10pm Sun; 🅿🖊)

Guy Fieri's Vegas
Kitchen & Bar   AMERICAN $$

Diners, Drive-ins and Dives celebrity chef Guy Fieri has opened his first restaurant on the Strip at LINQ Casino (see 1 Map p57, C5), dishing out an eclectic menu of his own design, inspired by many years journeying America's back roads for the best and fairest down-home cooking. (📞702-794-3139; www.caesars.com; LINQ Casino; mains $12-28; ⏱9am-midnight)

Grand Wok   CHINESE $$

Come to Grand Wok (see 3 Map p52, C7), in business for over 25 years serving some of the best pan-Asian dishes you'll find this side of the Far East. Try the garlic shrimp fried rice with dried scallops. Sensational. (📞702-891-7879; www.mgmgrand.com/en/restaurants.html;

Joël Robuchon (p60)

MGM Grand; mains $12-28; ⊙11am-10pm Sun-Thu, to 11pm Fri & Sat)

Burger Bar
AMERICAN $$

 18 Map p52, B8

Since when can a hamburger be worth $60? When it's built with Kobe beef, sautéed foie gras and truffle sauce: it's the Rossini burger, the signature sandwich of chef Hubert Keller. Most menu options are more down-to-earth – diners select their own gourmet burger toppings and pair them with skinny fries and a liquor-spiked milkshake or beer float. (☑702-632-9364; www.burger-bar.com; Shoppes at Mandalay Place; mains $10-60; ⊙11am-11pm Sun-Thu, to 1am Fri & Sat; ⓟ❄ⓘ)

Searsucker Las Vegas
GASTROPUB $$

Searsucker (see 4 ◉ Map p52, B5) is a heavy hitter serving punchy small plates and killer cocktails in casual, cowboy-tinged digs on Caesars (p54) gaming floor. Daily happy hour and a modern American menu that has something for everyone. (☑702-866-1800; www.searsucker.com/las-vegas; Caesars Palace; mains $12-32; ⊙5pm-midnight)

Peppermill
DINER $$

19 Map p52, D3

Slide into a crescent-shaped booth at this retro casino coffee shop and revel in the old-school Vegas atmosphere. You can eavesdrop on Nevada cowboys and downtown politicos digging into a gigantic late-night bite or early breakfast. For tropical tiki drinks, step into the Peppermill's Fireside Lounge (p66). (☎702-735-4177; www.peppermilllasvegas.com; 2985 S Las Vegas Blvd; mains $8-32; ⊙24hr)

China Poblano   FUSION $$

Noodles and tacos, together? An eye-catching fusion eatery (see 41 🔒 Map p52, B6) from chef José Andrés mixes two unlikely cuisines – Chinese and Mexican – in a lively, hipster-friendly space where the glow of neon signs brightens darkened booths and barstools. Inspired street-food riffs include duck-tongue tacos with lychee and red-chili-braised pork buns. (☎702-698-7900; www.chinapoblano.com; Cosmopolitan; shared plates $5-20; ⊙11:30am-11pm Sun-Thu, to 11:30pm Fri & Sat; P ❄ ✐)

Cravings   BUFFET $$

Not the very best, but far from the worst of the Strip's buffets, Cravings (see 11 ◉ Map p52, B4) will probably leave you feeling you got your money's worth, with 11 live-action cooking stations, Goose Island IPA on tap and life-changing chocolate croissant bread pudding for dessert. Rather eat in your room? Ask about the takeout special ($16) that lets you fill up a to-go box. (☎702-791-7111; www.mirage.com; Mirage; per adult $16-32, per child 5-10yr $12-22; ⊙7am-9pm Mon-Fri, from 8am Sat & Sun; P ❄ ✐ 👶)

Morimoto   FUSION $$$

Iron Chef Masaharu Morimoto's latest Vegas incarnation is in his eponymous showcase restaurant (see 3 ◉ Map 52, C7), which pays homage to his Japanese roots and the cuisine of this city that has propelled him to legend status around the world. Dining here is an experience in every possible way and, we think, worth every penny. (☎702-891-1111; www.mgmgrand.com; MGM Grand; mains $24-75; ⊙5-10pm)

Joël Robuchon   FRENCH $$$

The acclaimed 'Chef of the Century' leads the pack in the French culinary invasion of the Strip. Adjacent to the MGM Grand's (p54) high-rollers' gaming area, Robuchon's plush leather and velvet dining rooms (see 3 ◉ Map p C7) feel like a dinner party at a 1930s Paris mansion. Seasonal tasting menus promise the meal of a lifetime – and they often deliver. (☎702-891-7925; www.joel-robuchon.com/en; MGM Grand; tasting menus $120-425; ⊙5-10pm)

Restaurant Guy Savoy   FRENCH $$$

With Strip-view picture windows, this exclusive dining room (see 4 ◉ Map p52, B5) is the only US restaurant by three-star Michelin chef Guy Savoy. Both the culinary concepts and the prices reach heavenly heights. If you just want a small taste, perhaps of artichoke black-truffle soup or crispy-skinned sea bass, sit in the Cognac Lounge for drinks and nibbles. Dinner reservations are essential. (☎702-731-7286; www.guysavoy.com; Caesars Palace; mains $80-110, tasting menus $120-350; ⏱5:30-9:30pm Wed-Sun)

Border Grill

MEXICAN $$$

20 Map p52, B8

With colorful modern murals and views over Mandalay Bay Beach (p27), this festive eatery dishes up modern Mexican fare designed by chefs from Bravo's *Top Chef Masters* and the Food Network's *Too Hot Tamales*. Come for the weekend brunch of unlimited Latin-inspired tapas ($35) and bottomless mimosas (extra $15). Border Grill uses only hormone-free meat and sustainably caught seafood. Reservations helpful. (☎702-632-7403; www.bordergrill.com; Mandalay Bay; mains $17-36; ⏱11am-10pm Mon-Fri, from 10am Sat & Sun; 🅿︎🖉🖘)

Bazaar Meat

STEAK $$$

21 Map p52, D2

Controversial Spanish chef José Andrés is at the helm of SLS' headline restaurant that offers a twist on the traditional steakhouse, inventively blending disparate flavors and cultures with mouthwatering success. The meaty menu does have some seafood (including a raw bar) for pescatarians, but vegetarians will want to look elsewhere. (☎855-761-7757; www.slslasvegas.com/dining/bazaar-meat; SLS; mains $38-90; ⏱5:30-10pm Sun-Thu, to 11pm Fri & Sat; 🅿︎❄︎)

 Local Life
Wicked Spoon Buffet

Wicked Spoon (☎702-698-7870; www.cosmopolitanlasvegas.com; Cosmopolitan; per person $26-51; ⏱8am-2pm & 5-9pm Mon-Thu, 8am-10pm Fri & Sat, 8am-9pm Sun; 🛜🖘) makes casino buffets seem cool again, with freshly prepared temptations served on individual plates for you to grab and take back to your table. The spread has all the expected meat, sushi, seafood and desserts, but with global upgrades – think roasted bone marrow and a gelato bar. Weekend brunch adds unlimited champagne mimosas or Bloody Marys (surcharge $10).

Hash House a Go Go

AMERICAN $$$

Fill up on this SoCal import's 'twisted farm food' (see 1 ◉ Map p52, C5), which has to be seen to be believed. The pancakes are as big as tractor tires, while farm-egg scrambles and housemade hashes could knock over a cow. Meatloaf, pot pies, chicken 'n' biscuits and wild-boar sloppy joes are what's for dinner, but it's more popular for breakfast and brunch. (☎702-254-4646; www.hashhouseagogo. com; LINQ; mains breakfast & lunch $8-16, dinner $17-39; ⏱24hr, closed 11pm-7am last Wed of month; ❄︎🖘)

Le Village Buffet

BUFFET $$$

22 ✗✗ Map p52, C5

An incredible array of fruits and cheeses, a toasty range of breads and pastries, and macaroons for dessert make this one of the best-value buffets on the Strip. Distinct cooking stations are themed by France's various regions, with an emphasis on seafood. Breakfasts are excellent, and so are weekend brunches. (📞702-946-7000; Paris Las Vegas; buffet adult $22-34, child 4-8yr $13-20; ⏰7am-10pm; ✗✗)

Bacchanal

BUFFET $$$

As over-the-top as Caesars Palace's (p54) statuary of gods and goddesses, this is the Strip's most expansive and expensive buffet (see 4 Map p52, B5). An all-you-can-eat feast of king crab legs, housemade sushi and dim sum, oak-grilled BBQ, baked-to-order soufflés and more goes beyond what you could possibly taste in one sitting. Windows overlook the Garden of the Gods pools. (📞702-731-7928; www.caesars.com; Caesars Palace; buffet per adult $30-58, child 4-10yr $15-27; ⏰8am-10pm; P❄✗✗)

Golden Steer

STEAK $$$

23 ✗✗ Map p52, D1

The Rat Pack, Marilyn Monroe and Elvis all dined at this fabulously retro steakhouse with the steer's head out front. Soak up the vintage Vegas vibes. (📞702-384-4470; www.goldensteersteakhouselasvegas.com; 308 W Sahara Ave; mains $29-55; ⏰4:30-10:30pm; ✗; 💻SDX)

Top of the World

AMERICAN $$$

While taking in the cloud-level views at this revolving romantic roost (see 2 👁 Map p52, D1) perched atop the Stratosphere (p54) tower, smartly dressed diners enjoy impeccable service and satisfying, if overpriced, dishes such as Colorado rack of lamb dusted with Moroccan spices or California black cod swirled in Thai green curry sauce. Excellent wine list. Reservations essential. (📞702-380-7711; www.topoftheworldlv.com; Stratosphere; mains lunch $25-34, dinner $40-79; ⏰11am-11pm)

Rivea

EUROPEAN $$$

24 ✗✗ Map p52, B8

Atop Delano, Rivea's upscale French-Italian dining from celebrity chef Alain Ducasse, stands on its own, but the real pull here is the classy but casual atmosphere and the incomparable indoor and patio views of the Strip. (📞702-632-9500; www.delanolasvegas.com; Delano, Mandalay Bay; mains $24-72, tasting menus from $115; ⏰6-10pm)

Buffet at Wynn

BUFFET $$$

25 ✗✗ Map p52, C4

Wynn's (p48) buffet is an upscale version of the average all-you-can-eat feed on the Strip. A color palette of butter yellow, sea green and dusty rose, with floral arrangements bursting out of vases everywhere, lends some dignity to the gluttony of 15 live-action cooking stations, piles of cracked crab legs and an unlimited dessert bar. (📞702-770-

Luxor (p57)

3340; www.wynnlasvegas.com; Wynn; per person $32-60; ☺7:30am-9:30pm; 🄿 ❄ ✏ 👶)

Stripsteak

STEAK $$$

26 ⊗ Map p52, B8

Esquire magazine once named chef Michael Mina's butter-poached bone-in-top loin one of the USA's very best steaks. The chef's minimalist steak-house knifes into an exceptional menu of all-natural Angus and American Kobe beef, taste-awakening appetizers like ahi tuna and hamachi poppers, and classic side dishes with a twist, from truffle mac 'n' cheese to soy-glazed green beans. Reservations essential. (🄹702-632-7200; www.michaelmina.net; Mandalay Bay; mains $39-75; ☺4-10pm)

Nobu

JAPANESE, FUSION $$$

Iron Chef Matsuhisa's sequel to his NYC establishment (see 4 ⊙ Map p52, B5) is almost as good as the original. The setting is postmodern Zen, with glowing yellow lanterns, private dining 'pods' and sociable *teppanyaki* grill tables. Stick with Nobu's classics such as black cod with miso, South American–influenced *tiradito* (a lighter version of ceviche), spicy edamame and fusion sushi rolls. Reservations essential. (🄹702-785-6628; www.noburestaurants.com; Caesars Palace; shared plates $5-60, lunch mains $22-50, dinner tasting menus $90-500; ☺5-11pm Sun-Thu, to midnight Sat & Sun)

Top Tip
Getting into Nightclubs

Before braving a club's velvet rope and shelling out big bucks for the cover charge, look for the club's own promoters, usually standing on the casino floor of the corresponding hotel or resort – they're giving out expedited entry and free drinks passes, especially to well-dressed women. Alternatively, book ahead with a club promoter such as Chris Hornak of **Free Vegas Club Passes** (www.freevegasclubpasses.com).

Spice Market Buffet   BUFFET $$$

27 ✕ Map p52, C6

Middle Eastern, Asian, Italian and Mexican fare are thrown into the global mix at this jewel of a buffet, a throwback to the original Aladdin resort. Attentive service, above-average desserts and live-action cooking stations justify the often very long waits to be seated. (✆702-785-5555; Planet Hollywood; buffet adult $22-36, child 4-12yr $13-20; ⊙7am-11pm; ✈ ♿)

Todd English's Olives
MEDITERRANEAN $$$

28 ✕ Map p52, B5

East Coast chef Todd English pays homage to the ancient life-giving fruit at this Italian-inflected eatery. Flatbread pizza, housemade pasta and grilled meats get top billing. The chef's table faces a bustling open kitchen,

while the patio overlooks Lake Como. With an exceptional wine list and flamboyant desserts, it's always packed – come for lunch but, even then, make reservations first. (✆702-693-8181; www.toddenglish.com; Bellagio; mains lunch $17-29, dinner $25-49; ⊙restaurant 11am-2:45pm & 5-10:30pm, bar 3-5pm; P ✈)

Buffet at Bellagio   BUFFET $$$

29 ✕ Map p52, B5

Bellagio once competed for honors among Vegas' live-action buffets, but lately it has become second-tier. It's most satisfying at breakfast or lunch. The more varied dinnertime spread features seafood and creative dishes from around the world – too bad they don't all taste as good as they look. (✆702-693-8865; www.bellagio.com; Bellagio; per person $24-46; ⊙7am-10pm; P ❄)

Drinking

Hakkasan   CLUB

At this lavish Asian-inspired nightclub (see 3 ◉ Map p52, C7), international jet-set DJs like Tiësto and Steve Aoki rule the jam-packed main dance floor bordered by VIP booths and floor-to-ceiling LED screens. More offbeat sounds spin in the intimate Ling Ling Club, revealing leather sofas and backlit amber glass. Bouncers enforce the dress code: upscale nightlife attire (no athletic wear, collared shirts required for men). (✆702-891-3838; www.hakkasanlv.com; MGM Grand; cover $20-75; ⊙10pm-4am Wed-Sun)

Parasol Down (p50), Wynn

Omnia
CLUB

30 ⊙ Map p52, B5

Hakkasan group's new Caesars mega-club offers Top 40/hip-hop DJs, plus bottle service and Strip views with a Miami Beach vibe. Residencies by Calvin Harris, Steve Aoki and Martin Garrix. (www.omnianightclub.com; Caesars Palace; cover female/male $20/40; ⊙10pm-4am Tue & Thu-Sun)

Marquee
CLUB

The Cosmopolitan's (p37) glam nightclub (see 41 🔒 Map p52, B6) cashes in on its multimillion-dollar sound system and a happening dancefloor surrounded by towering LED screens displaying light projections that complement EDM tracks hand-picked by famous-name DJs. From late spring through early fall, Marquee's mega-popular daytime pool club heads outside to a lively party deck overlooking the Strip, with VIP cabanas and bungalows. (☎702-333-9000; www.marqueelasvegas.com; Cosmopolitan; ⊙10pm-5am Mon, Fri & Sat)

Jewel
CLUB

31 ⊙ Map p52, B6

From the creators of Hakkasan, long-awaited Jewel replaces its predecessor Haze, which failed to dazzle. Boasting five VIP suites (because it's all about being seen) and over 1400 sq ft of shimmering LED ribbon lighting,

Jewel, despite accommodating up to 2000 revelers, is pitched as an 'intimate' alternative to the Strip's megaclubs. Monday nights offer locals free admission. (☑702-590-8000; www. jewelnightclub.com; Aria; cover female/male from $20/30; ⊘10:30am-4am Fri, Sat & Mon)

XS   CLUB

 32 Map p52, C3

XS is *the* hottest nightclub in Vegas – at least for now. Its extravagantly gold-drenched decor and over-the-top design mean you'll be waiting in line for cocktails at a bar towered over by ultra-curvaceous, larger-than-life golden statues of female torsos. Famous-name electronica DJs make the dancefloor writhe, while high rollers opt for VIP bottle service at private poolside cabanas. (☑702-770-0097; www.xslasvegas.com; Encore; cover $20-50; ⊘10pm-4am Fri & Sat, from 9:30pm Sun, from 10:30pm Mon)

Surrender   CLUB

33 Map p52, C3

Even the club-averse admit that this is an audaciously gorgeous place to hang out, with its saffron-colored silk walls, mustard banquettes, bright yellow patent leather entrance and a shimmering wall-art snake coiled behind the bar. Play blackjack or just hang out by the pool after dark during summer. EDM and hip-hop DJs and musicians pull huge crowds. (☑702-770-7300; www.surrendernightclub.com; Encore; cover $20-40; ⊘10:30pm-4am Wed, Fri & Sat)

Wet Republic   CLUB

Think of Wet Republic (see 3 ◎ Map p52 C7), the city's biggest 'ultra pool,' as a nightclub brought out into the sunlight. The mostly 20- and 30-something crowd in stylish swimwear show up for EDM tunes spun by megawatt DJs like Calvin Harris, fruity cocktails and bobbing oh-so-coolly around saltwater pools while checking out the bikini-clad scenery. Book ahead for VIP bungalows, daybeds and cabanas. (☑702-891-3563; www.wetrepublic.com; MGM Grand; cover $20-40; ⊘11am-5pm Mon & Thu-Sun)

107 SkyLounge   LOUNGE

There's just no place to get any higher in Las Vegas – without the approval of an air traffic controller – than the lounge overlooking the revolving Top of the World (p62) restaurant (see 2 ◎ Map p52, D1). Come during happy hour (4pm to 7pm daily) for two-for-one cocktails, half-price appetizers and striking sunset views. (☑702-380-7711; www.topoftheworldlv.com/level107.php; 2000 S Las Vegas Blvd, 107th fl, Stratosphere Tower; ⊘4pm-4am)

Fireside Lounge   LOUNGE

Don't be blinded by the outlandishly bright neon outside. The Strip's most spellbinding retro hideaway (see 19 Map p52, D3) awaits at the pint-sized Peppermill (p59) casino. Courting couples adore the sunken fire pit, fake tropical foliage and 64oz goblet-sized 'Scorpion' cocktails served by waiters

Encore Beach Club

in black evening gowns. (☏702-735-7635; www.peppermilllasvegas.com; 2985 S Las Vegas Blvd, Peppermill; ⊘24hr; ☒Deuce)

Drai's Beachclub & Nightclub
CLUB

34 📍 Map p52, C5

Feel ready for an after-hours party scene straight outta Hollywood? Or maybe you just wanna hang out all day poolside, then shake your booty on the dancefloor while DJs spin hip-hop, mash-ups and electronica? This club has you covered pretty much all day and night. Dress to kill: no sneakers, tank tops or baggy jeans. (☏702-777-3800; www.draislv.com; Cromwell Las Vegas;

nightclub cover $20-50; ⊘nightclub 10pm-5am Thu-Sun, beach club 11am-6pm Fri-Sun)

Encore Beach Club
CLUB

35 📍 Map p52, C3

Soak up sunshine on a larger-than-life 'lilypad,' bob around the pool to DJ-spun tunes, play high-stakes blackjack by the pool or kick back in a private bungalow or a cabana with its own hot tub. The club features three tiered pools (one with an island platform for dancing), plus a gaming pavilion and top international DJs. (☏702-770-7300; www.encorebeachclub.com; Encore; cover $30-40; ⊘10pm-4am Thu, 11am-7pm Fri & Sun, from 10am Sat)

Top Tip
Cashless Rides

Cashless rideshare services booked through your smartphone (such as Use Uber and Lyft) are the cheapest, most convenient and most efficient way to get around Vegas. There's a glut of eager drivers trying to outshine each other for your post-ride five-star ratings, picking you up in spotless chariots, and often offering bottled water and tailored playlists in surround sound.

Chandelier Lounge   COCKTAIL BAR

Towering high in the center of Cosmopolitan (p37), this ethereally designed cocktail bar (see 41 🔒 Map p52, B6) is inventive yet beautifully simple, with three levels connected by romantic curved staircases, all draped with glowing strands of glass beads. The second level is headquarters for molecular mixology (order a martini made with liquid nitrogen), while the third specializes in floral and fruit infusions. (📞702-698-7979; www.cosmopolitanlasvegas.com/lounges-bars/chandelier; Cosmopolitan; ⏱24hr; 🚌Deuce)

Mandarin Bar & Tea Lounge   LOUNGE

36 🍸 Map p52, C6

With glittering Strip views from the panoramic windows of the hotel's 23rd-floor 'sky lobby,' this sophisticated lounge serves exotic teas by day and champagne cocktails by night. Make reservations for afternoon tea (from \$36, available 1pm to 5pm daily). (📞702-590-8888; www.mandarinoriental.com; Mandarin Oriental, CityCenter; ⏱lounge 10am-10pm daily, bar noon-2am Fri & Sat, 4pm-1am Sun-Thu)

Entertainment

Blue Man Group   LIVE PERFORMANCE

Art, music and technology combine with a dash of comedy in one of Vegas' most popular, family-friendly shows (see 10 ◉ Map p52, B8) at Luxor (p57). (📞702-262-4400; www.blueman.com; Luxor; tickets \$80-190; ⏱7pm & 9:30pm; 👫)

Beatles LOVE   THEATER

Another smash hit from Cirque du Soleil, *Beatles LOVE* (see 11 ◉ Map p52, B4) started as the brainchild of the late George Harrison. Using *Abbey Road* master tapes, the show psychedelically fuses the musical legacy of the Beatles with Cirque's high-energy dancers and signature aerial acrobatics. Come early to photograph the trippy, rainbow-colored entryway and grab drinks at Abbey Road bar, next to Revolution Lounge. (📞702-792-7777; www.cirquedusoleil.com; Mirage; tickets \$79-180; ⏱7pm & 9:30pm Thu-Mon; 👫)

Understand

Gangster History

In 1941, Los Angles hotelier Thomas Hull opened Vegas' first casino hotel, El Rancho Vegas, inspiring mobster Benjamin 'Bugsy' Siegel to build an even more luxurious resort in the desert that would draw high rollers from all over the world.

Bugsy & the Flamingo

Backed by East Coast mob money, Siegel took over LA-nightclub-owner and *Hollywood Reporter*-publisher Billy Wilkerson's bankrupt construction project and opened the $6 million Flamingo casino hotel in 1946. With its pastel paint job, tuxedo-clad janitors, Hollywood entertainers and neon signs, the Flamingo became the model for the Las Vegas high life to come.

The Fabulous Fifties

In 1950, following a lavish opening party for the Desert Inn (primarily owned by Moe Dalitz, head of a Cleveland-based crime syndicate), a full-blown federal investigation made a disturbing trend crystal clear: the Vegas casino industry had deep ties to mobsters from across the nation. The mob loved Las Vegas. It gave them a legitimacy and a glamorous cachet they had never experienced before. And by fixing the games, bribing local politicians and skimming profits both under and over the table, they were getting rich fast.

Frank Sinatra and his Rat Pack pals helped build this town. They weren't merely legendary headliners; they were also the darlings of gossip columns from LA to New York, and their all-night partying and tumultuous lives entertained millions. Their antics at the Sands casino hotel brought adoring fans, movie stars and famous politicians to Las Vegas by the planeload.

From Mobsters to Megaresorts

In the 1960s, federal and state regulators made an effort to clean up the gambling industry. Scandals plagued the casinos, as charges of corruption, racketeering, influence peddling and tax evasion were investigated by federal agencies – all the bad publicity was hurting tourism. Industrialist Howard Hughes and, later, hotshot Steve Wynn added an air of legitimacy to the scene with their investments and construction of new casino resorts.

Top Tip

Last-Minute Tickets

Tix 4 Tonight (☎877-849-4868; www.tix4tonight.com; 3200 S Las Vegas Blvd, Fashion Show Mall; ⊗10am-8pm) offers half-price tickets for a limited lineup of same-day shows and small discounts on 'always sold-out' shows. It's located outside Neiman Marcus department store. Check the website for other locations.

Criss Angel Mindfreak Live
 LIVE PERFORMANCE

Find out why Criss Angel is the most watched magician in history in what is billed as the greatest magic spectacle (see 10 ⊙ Map p52, B8) of all time. Seeing is believing! (☎702-262-4400; www.luxor.com; Luxor; ⊗shows 7pm & 9:30pm Wed-Sun)

T-Mobile Arena
CONCERT VENUE

37 ⭐ Map p52, B7

New in 2016 and costing a cool $375 million, Las Vegas' premier stadium occupies a prime spot on the Strip and boasts 24 private boxes, 54 suites and seating for up to 20,000 people. (☎702-692-1600; www.t-mobilearena.com; 3780 S Las Vegas Blvd; ⊗box office noon-6pm)

Park Theater
CONCERT VENUE

38 ⭐ Map p52, C7

Stage one of **Monte Carlo's** (☎702-730-7777; www.montecarlo.com; 3770 S

Las Vegas Blvd; ⊗24hr; P) rebranding as Park MGM, this state-of-the-art 5000-plus-seat concert venue is Vegas' newest, opened in December 2016. (☎844-600-7275; 3770 S Las Vegas Blvd; ticket prices vary; ⊗box office 9am-6pm)

Colosseum
LIVE PERFORMANCE

A high-tech version of ancient Rome's famous arena, this spectacular 4100-seat venue (see 4 ⊙ Map p52, B5) has state-of-the-art sound and lighting systems fit for the first-class performers who take the stage here, including Celine Dion, Elton John and Jerry Seinfeld. Thanks to the circular layout, there's hardly a bad seat in the house, with the audience seated no further than 120ft from the stage. (☎866-227-5938; www.thecolosseum.com; Caesars Palace; tickets $55-500)

Carrot Top
COMEDY

Even if his TV commercials annoyed you to death, this wild and curly orange-haired comedian's shtick could leave your side split and your gut busted. The fast-paced show (see 10 ⊙ Map p52, B8) runs the audience ragged with physical props, dark and twisted stand-up humor and merciless skewering of pop stars, Hollywood celebs and politicians. (☎702-262-4400; www.luxor.com; Luxor; tickets $50; ⊗8pm Mon & Wed-Sun)

Shops at Crystals

Shopping

Shops at Crystals
MALL

39 Map p52, C6

Design-conscious Crystals is the most striking shopping center on the Strip. Win big at blackjack? Waltz inside Christian Dior, Dolce & Gabbana, Prada, Hermès, Harry Winston, Paul Smith or Stella McCartney showrooms at CityCenter's (p36) shrine to haute couture. For sexy couples with unlimited cash to burn, Kiki de Montparnasse is a one-stop shop for lingerie and bedroom toys. (www.crystalsatcitycenter. com; 3720 S Las Vegas Blvd, CityCenter; 10am-11pm Sun-Thu, to midnight Fri & Sat)

Fashion Show
MALL

40 Map p52, C4

Nevada's largest mall is an eye-catcher: topped off by 'the Cloud,' a silver multimedia canopy resembling a flamenco hat, Fashion Show harbors more than 250 chain shops and department stores. Hot European additions to the mainstream lineup include British clothier Topshop (and Topman for men). Live runway shows happen hourly from noon to 5pm on Friday, Saturday and Sunday. (702-369-8382; www.thefashion-show.com; 3200 S Las Vegas Blvd; 10am-9pm Mon-Sat, 11am-7pm Sun;)

Top Tip
Dressing for Vegas

Dress to impress, whether you're 40-something and doing the rounds of celebrity chefs, or a youngster hitting Drai's beach club. Ladies, you want to look ravishing. Guys, you need to look schmick. Dress codes (collared shirts for men, and no athletic wear or hats) often exist and are enforced. If you want to explore the Strip, wear comfortable shoes. Also, bring loose, cool clothing for the summer heat. Vegas is warm to hot for much of the year, but it can get cold quickly in fall and winter, so be prepared.

Shops at Cosmopolitan
FASHION & ACCESSORIES

41   Map p52, B6

Hipster-loving boutiques gather inside the Cosmopolitan (p37) resort: CRSVR sneaker boutique, DNA2050 denim bar, AllSaints Spitalfields from the UK, Molly Brown's swimwear, Retrospecs & Co eyewear, Skins 6|2 Cosmetics and Kidrobot for DIY toys and pop-culture collectibles. Rent the Runway can be a lifesaver for women who forgot to pack the right dress for a big night out (bachelorette parties welcome). (www.cosmopolitanlasvegas.com/shopping; Cosmopolitan; ☉10am-11pm)

Shops at Forum
MALL

42   Map p52, B5

Caesars' (p54) fanciful nod to ancient Roman marketplaces houses 160 designer emporia, including catwalk wonders Armani, DKNY, Jimmy Choo, John Varvatos and Versace; trend-setting jewelry and accessory stores; and one-of-a-kind specialty boutiques such as Agent Provocateur lingerie, Bettie Page pin-up fashions, MAC cosmetics and Kiehl's bath-and-body shop. Don't miss the spiral escalator, a grand entrance for divas strutting off the Strip. (www.simon.com/mall/the-forum-shops-at-caesars-palace/stores; Caesars Palace; ☉10am-11pm Sun-Thu, to midnight Fri & Sat)

Miracle Mile Shops
MALL

43   Map p52, C6

This sleekly redesigned shopping mall is still a staggering 1.2 miles long. With 170 retailers, the focus is on contemporary chains, especially urban apparel, jewelry and gifts. Standout shops include Bettie Page for 1940s and '50s pinup and vintage-style dresses; Swedish import H&M; LA denim king True Religion; and Vegas' own rock-star boutique, Stash, for both women and men. (☎702-866-0704; www.miraclemileshopslv.com; Planet Hollywood; ☉10am-11pm Sun-Thu, to midnight Fri & Sat)

COURTESY OF MIRACLE MILE SHOPS ©

Miracle Mile Shops

Houdini's Magic Shop   TOYS

44 🔒 Map p52, C6

Let yourself be roped into this real-deal magic shop by the staff who perform illusions and card tricks out front for sometimes inebriated passersby (they're easy targets). Magician memorabilia and DIY magic kits are sold inside. Check the website for other locations in Vegas. (☎702-798-4789; www.houdini.com; Miracle Mile Shops; ⏰9am-midnight Mon-Thu & Sun, to 1am Fri & Sat)

Bonanza Gift Shop   GIFTS & SOUVENIRS

45 🔒 Map p52, D1

The self-proclaimed 'purveyors of Las Vegas pop culture' brag about running the world's largest gift shop. Whether or not it's true, it's a blast wading through the truly terrible, 100% tacky selection of souvenirs. Beware that prices for kitsch are higher here than at Downtown's Fremont Street Experience (p111). (☎702-385-7359; www.worldslargestgift-shop.com; 2440 S Las Vegas Blvd; ⏰8am-midnight)

Explore

East of the Strip

Visits east reward explorers with a deeper understanding of what makes Vegas tick. You won't find many top sights here, but there are a few, like collections of vintage pinball machines, rock-and-roll memorabilia and a glimpse into Las Vegas' dark atomic past. You'll also find cheap eats, bars where bartenders drink and LGBT haunts.

The Sights in a Day

Wake up late – this is Vegas. Revisit your childhood at the **Pinball Hall of Fame** (p84), a hole-in-the-wall vintage gaming showcase filled with old-school pinball, video arcade and carnival sideshow games, all dating from the 1940s to the '90s.

Go for an authentic Mexican lunch at cozy **Lindo Michoacan** (p86) before heading to the **National Atomic Testing Museum** (p80) to learn about the region's 1950s heyday as an atomic testing site. Gamblers and tourists downtown used to stare, mesmerized, as mushroom clouds rose behind Fremont St – the city even crowned a Miss Atomic Bomb.

If there's any reason Vegas partygoers detour east of the Strip, it's the fashionable **Hard Rock Hotel & Casino** (p76) with its cool eateries, high-tech music venues and world-class rock-'n'-roll memorabilia. Stroll through the casino to admire the museum-like collection of rock stars' guitars and leather jackets, then catch a show at **Joint** (p87). Leave the Hard Rock to have drinks and observe the locals in their natural habitat on the patio at nearby **Firefly** (p85).

Top Sights

Hard Rock Hotel & Casino (p76)

National Atomic Testing Museum (p80)

Best of Las Vegas

Off-Strip Dining

Firefly (p85)

Lotus of Siam (p85)

Culinary Dropout (p77)

Local Culture

National Atomic Testing Museum (p80)

Pinball Hall of Fame (p84)

Casinos

Hard Rock Hotel & Casino (p76)

Getting There

🚌 **Bus** No 108 southbound from Paradise Rd.

🚕 **Taxi** Around $15, plus tip, to the Strip; $20 to Downtown.

Top Sights
Hard Rock Hotel & Casino

The Hard Rock's sexy, see-and-be-seen scene is perfect for rock stars and entourage wannabes alike. Especially favored by southern Californians, this party hotel opens onto a circular casino with a competitive spread of table games, a state-of-the-art race and sports book, a busy poker room and the glowing Peacock high-limit gaming salon.

Map p82; C6

📞 702-693-5000

www.hardrockhotel.com

4455 Paradise Rd

🕐 24hr

🚌 108

Rehab Beach Club

Rock-and-Roll Memorabilia

The world's original rock-and-roll casino houses what may be the most impressive collection of rock-star memorabilia ever assembled under one roof. Priceless items being watched over by security guards suited up like bouncers are concert attire once worn by Elvis, Britney Spears and Prince; a display case filled with Beatles mementos; Jim Morrison's handwritten lyrics to one of the Doors' greatest hits; and dozens of leather jackets and guitars formerly owned by everyone from the Ramones to U2.

Culinary Dropout

With a pool-view patio and live bands rocking on weekends, there's no gastropub more awesome than Hard Rock's legendary **Culinary Dropout** (702-522-8100; mains brunch $8-14, lunch & dinner $14-32; 11am-11pm Mon-Thu, 11am-midnight Fri, 9am-midnight Sat, 9am-11pm Sun). Dip warm pretzels in provolone fondue or homemade potato chips in onion dip, then bite into fried chicken and honey biscuits, while downing pints of amber nectar...no, not all at the same time. Though, if you wanted to, nobody here would hold it against you.

Rehab Beach Club

There's seasonal swim-up blackjack and general mayhem at the Rehab Beach Club, open to the public Thursdays to Sundays from 11am to 6pm and for looser, more chilled-out Mondays (same times). You might spot A-list celebs, rock stars and costumed partyers among the hordes lounging poolside. The original, and some would say the best, these guys are the ones responsible for Vegas' daytime pool-club obsession.

☑ Top Tips

▶ Pace yourself. If you favor rock over EDM, Hard Rock is your holy grail. Don't burn out too soon, though! You don't want to be 'that person' slumped in the corner. Not here.

▶ Well-priced, recently renovated rooms make basing yourself at Hard Rock an appealing proposition for music lovers.

▶ There's a free shuttle between Hard Rock and the Strip, for hotel guests only.

✗ Take a Break

If you've sampled all of Hard Rock's eats and you need an incognito quick fix, head up the road to Fat Choy (p84).

For something a little more substantial along an Asian theme, and a little further afield, Lotus of Siam (p85) offers the best Thai food we've found in the Mojave.

BURWELL PHOTOGRAPHY/GETTY IMAGES ©

Tacos

Live Music at Joint

Concerts at Joint (p87), Hard Rock's scaled-down music venue (for just 4000 people), feel intimate – even when Aerosmith, Coldplay or Morrissey are in town. Most shows here are standing-room only, with VIP balcony seats (reservation only) upstairs. Other on-site venues include a cozy music (and comedy) lounge called Vinyl and the floating poolside Palapa Bar.

Pink Taco

The Mexican food served here may have Californicated, but that makes it even better. **Pink Taco** (✆702-693-5525; mains $14-21; ⏱11am-10pm Mon-Thu, to late Fri & Sat, 11am-10pm Sun) is essentially a Baja fish-taco shack crossed with a Sunset Strip tequila bar. It's one of several excellent casual eateries at Hard Rock, a refreshing change from the higher-end dining options found on the Strip.

Reliquary Spa & Salon

Retreat to this aquatic **sanctuary** (✆salon 702-693-5522, spa 702-693-5520; spa & fitness center day pass hotel guests/nonguests $25/50; ⏱spa 8am-7pm, salon 10am-7pm Tue-Sat, 10am-5pm Sun & Mon), where you can let that pesky hangover melt away as you bliss out with a Thai fusion massage or a 'Cloud Nine' facial while sipping on a freshly squeezed concoction from the juice bar. Rockstar makeovers happen in the salon.

BIR FOTOS/ALAMY STOCK PHOTO ©

Hard Rock Hotel & Casino

Top Sights
National Atomic Testing Museum

The multimedia exhibits here focus on science, technology and the social history of the 'Atomic Age,' which lasted from WWII until atmospheric bomb testing was driven underground in 1961. A worldwide ban on nuclear testing was declared in 1992. Examine southern Nevada's nuclear past, present and future, from Native American traditions to the environmental legacy of atomic testing today.

⊙ Map p82; C5

☏ 702-794-5151

www.nationalatomictesting-museum.org

755 Flamingo Rd E, Desert Research Institute; 🚌 202

adult/child $22/16

🕒 10am-5pm Mon-Sat, noon-5pm Sun

Science & Technology Exhibits

As you make your way through the museum's permanent exhibits, take time to inspect at least a few of the 12,000 historical artifacts collected from the earliest days of atomic testing through to nuclear science today. Learn the history of how the first atomic bomb was developed, and also how atmospheric and underground testing differ. An eye-catching gallery of radiation trackers registers the sobering truth about the dangers of nuclear weapons testing.

Cultural Exhibits

This Smithsonian-affiliated museum also explores the influence of atomic testing on society. Displays show what everyday life was like for Americans during the Cold War, when 'duck and cover' nuclear-bomb drills took place in elementary schools and Nevadans watched mushroom clouds bloom over the desert. Contemporary exhibits look at the environmental costs of atomic weapons, as well as Native American perspectives on land use and nuclear power.

Ticket Booth

Near the museum's front entrance, the ticket booth is a replica of a historical guard station from the Nevada Test Site, where atomic bomb testing began in 1951. Some of the museum volunteers who staff the ticket booth once worked at the site.

Nevada National Security Site

Guided bus tours of the **Nevada National Security Site** (☎702-295-0944; www.nv.energy.gov/outreach/tours.aspx; admission free) depart from the museum, generally at least once a month. You'll usually get to see surviving structures from the 1950s atomic testing era and moon-like craters that are many football fields wide. Apply online for tour reservations as far in advance as possible.

☑ Top Tips

▶ Combine a visit to the museum with some local cheap eats – there's plenty to savor.

▶ Uber and Lyft are your friends and by far the easiest way to get to the museum and your subsequent destination (lunch nearby?).

▶ Apply online for tours of the fascinating, high-security Nevada National Security Site as far in advance as possible (weeks or months advised).

✗ Take a Break

Any time is a good time for tapas, and you're less than a mile away from some of the best Spanish and Latin American dining in town, at locals' prices. Make a beeline for Firefly (p85).

One of the best vegan/vegetarian joints in town, Rainbow's End Cafe (p84), is found in this neck of the woods.

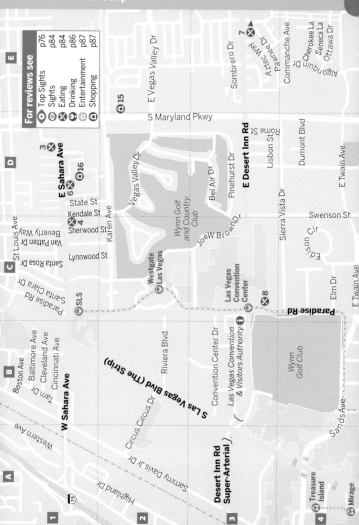

For reviews see

⊙	Top Sights	p76
⊙	Sights	p84
⊗	Eating	p84
⊗	Drinking	p86
⊕	Entertainment	p87
⊛	Shopping	p87

Algonquin Dr

10

Tamarus St

Caliente St

Rochelle Ave

11

Escondido St

University Ave

E Harmon Ave

Hialeh Dr

114th Dr

Santa Anita Dr

Roberta St

1

Lorilyn Ave

Dorothy Ave

Elizabeth Ave

Pinball Hall
of Fame

Caliente St

E Reno Ave

Tamarus St

Escondido St

E

S Maryland Pkwy

Cambridge St

E Flamingo Rd

Cottage Grove Ave

University of
Nevada,
Las Vegas
(UNLV)

University Rd

Lulu Ave

Toni Ave

Wilbur St

De Met Dr

Hacienda Ave

Swenson St

National Atomic
Testing Museum

Tropicana Wash

Viking Rd

Fredrika Dr

Swenson St

9

13

12

Naples Dr

Paradise Rd

Palo Verde Rd

Rent A Car Rd

14

D

C

McCarran
International
Airport

0.5 miles

1 km

Howard Hughes Pkwy

Flamingo Wash

Westchester Dr

Vegas
Mob Tour

E Flamingo Rd

Charlotte Dr

2

Hard Rock

Rochelle Ave

Lana Ave

E Harmon Ave

Deckow La

Koval La

E Tropicana Ave

B

Ida Ave

Winnick Ave

Albert Ave

Harrah's/
The LINQ

Flamingo/
Caesars
Palace

Bally's/Paris
Las Vegas

Audrie St

MGM
Grand

E Reno Ave

0

0.5 miles

1 km

N

A

Excalibur

Luxor

Giles St

Mandalay
Bay

S Las Vegas Blvd (The Strip)

THE STRIP

5

6

7

8

Sights

Pinball Hall of Fame   MUSEUM

1 ⊙ Map p82, E7

You may have more fun at this arcade than playing the Strip's slot machines. Tim Arnold shares his collection of 200-plus vintage pinball and video games; take time to read the handwritten cards explaining the unusual history behind the restored machines. (☑702-597-2627; www.pinballmuseum.org; 1610 E Tropicana Ave; per game 25¢-$1; ⊙11am-11pm Sun-Thu, to midnight Fri & Sat; 🚼; 🚌201)

Vegas Mob Tour   BUS

2 ⊙ Map p82, B5

Created with input from real-life mobsters and historians, this bus tour delves into Sin City's underworld past, including celebrity scandals, mobster assassinations and other dirty laundry. Tickets include pizza and admission to Downtown's Mob Museum (p102). By reservation only. (☑702-677-9015; www. vegasmobtour.com; 255 E Flamingo Rd, Tuscany Suites; 3hr tour $90)

Eating

Rainbow's End Cafe   HEALTH FOOD $

3 🍴 Map p82, D1

Vegans and vegetarians rejoice! It's not as classy as the steakhouses of the Strip, nor is its menu any more substantial, but the food here is wholesome, fresh and certified organic wherever possible. (☑702-737-1338; www. facebook.com/rainbowsendlv/; 1100 E Sahara Ave #120; light meals $6-13; ⊙10am-7pm Mon-Fri, to 6pm Sat, to 4pm Sun; 🅿🛜🍴)

Fat Choy   FUSION $

4 🍴 Map p82, C1

Classic American diner meets Asian comfort food in this tiny space within the tidy Eureka locals' casino. (☑702-794-3464; http://fatchoylv.com; 595 E Sahara Ave, Eureka Casino; mains $7-12; ⊙11am-10pm Mon-Thu, to midnight Sat, 9am-10pm Sun)

Understand
You Can Leave Your Hat On

Vegas is the original adult Disneyland. Prostitution may be illegal, but there are plenty of places offering the illusion of sex on demand. Unescorted women are not welcome at most 'gentleman's clubs,' especially not on busy nights. Bring cash for tips. Most strip clubs sit in industrial areas west of the Strip and I-15 Fwy. The largest is **Sapphire** (Map p82, A2; ☑702-796-6000; www.sapphirelasvegas. com; 3025 Sammy Davis Jr Dr; cover $30-50; ⊙24hr), with a stable of thousands of entertainers and VIP skyboxes overlooking a showroom dominated by a story-high martini glass. Beefy men strip upstairs on Friday and Saturday nights.

Margarita and mojito

Firefly
TAPAS $$

5 Map p82, C5

Firefly is always packed with a fashionable local crowd, who come for well-prepared Spanish and Latin American tapas, such as *patatas bravas,* chorizo-stuffed empanadas and vegetarian bites like garbanzo beans seasoned with chili, lime and sea salt. A back-lit bar dispenses the house specialty sangria – red, white or sparkling – and fruity mojitos. Reservations strongly recommended. (📞702-369-3971; www.fireflylv.com; 3824 Paradise Rd; shared plates $5-12, mains $15-20; ⊙11:30am-1am Mon-Thu, to 2am Fri & Sat, 10am-1am Sun; 🚌108)

Lotus of Siam
THAI $$

6 Map p82, D1

Saipin Chutima's authentic northern Thai cooking has won almost as many awards as her distinguished European and New World wine cellar. Critics have suggested this might be America's best Thai restaurant and we're sure it's up there with the best. Although the strip-mall hole-in-the-wall may not look like much, foodies flock here. Reservations essential. (📞702-735-3033; www.lotusofsiamlv.com; 953 E Sahara Ave; mains $9-30; ⊙11am-2:30pm Mon-Fri, 5:30-10pm daily; 🍴; 🚌SDX)

Double Down Saloon

This dark, psychedelic gin joint appeals to the lunatic fringe. **Double Down Saloon** (Map p82, C6; ☎702-791-5775; www.doubledownsaloon. com; 4640 Paradise Rd; ⊙24hr; ▢108) never closes, there's never a cover charge, the house drink is called 'ass juice' and it claims to be the birthplace of the bacon martini. When live bands aren't terrorizing the crowd, the jukebox vibrates with New Orleans jazz, British punk, Chicago blues and surf-guitar.

Lindo Michoacan   MEXICAN $$

 7 Map p82, E3

Handmade ceramics and faux adobe walls make this hideout feel far from the Strip. Family recipes fill the huge menu of Mexican classics, including seafood, *nopalito* (cactus) salad, beef *lengua* (tongue) and *menudo* (tripe and hominy soup). Call ahead for free shuttle service from the convention center's monorail station. (☎702-735-6828; www. lindomichoacan.com; 2655 E Desert Inn Rd; mains $13-24; ⊙10am-11pm; ♿; ▢203)

Envy   STEAK $$$

8 Map p82, C3

A dramatic entrance leads inside where power brokers recline on high-backed chairs amid boldly colored paintings and theatrical curtains. The signature steaks and wine cellar get unfailingly high marks, with gourmet side dishes like bourbon creamed corn. It's next door to the city's convention center. Reservations recommended. (☎702-784-5700; www.envysteakhouse.com; 3400 Paradise Rd, Renaissance Las Vegas; mains $29-58; ⊙5-10pm; ♿; ▢Convention Center)

Drinking

Hofbräuhaus   BAR

9 ▣ Map p82, C6

This Bavarian beer hall and garden replicates the Munich original. Celebrate Oktoberfest year-round with premium imports, fair *Fräuleins* and live oompah bands nightly. (☎702-853-2337; www. hofbrauhauslasvegas.com; 4510 Paradise Rd; ⊙11am-11pm Sun-Thu, to midnight Fri & Sat)

Flair Nightclub   GAY & LESBIAN

10 ▣ Map p82, E5

Vegas' premier LGBT venue has three bars and an outdoor patio. (☎702-733-8787; www.flairvegas.com; 1700 E Flamingo Rd; ⊙10pm-4am Thu-Sun)

Garage   GAY

11 ▣ Map p82, E5

One of Vegas' largest and most popular gay bars. (☎702-440-6333; www. thegaragelv.com; 1487 E Flamingo Rd; ⊙24hr)

Piranha   GAY & LESBIAN

12 ▣ Map p82, C7

The gay universe of the Fruit Loop orbits Sin City's sexiest gay nightclub, decked out with fireplace patios, aquariums and waterfalls, plus the luxurious 8½ Ultra Lounge. Expect outrageous theme parties, drag queen bingo, and ladies-only and Latin nights. (📞702-791-0100; www.piranhavegas.com; 4633 Paradise Rd; cover free-$20; ⏱24hr; 🚌108)

Freezone
GAY & LESBIAN

 13 Map p82, C7

Every night is a party at this gay dive bar. Sunday is ladies' night with go-go girls, Thursday is boyz' night with go-go boys, Friday and Saturday nights feature drag cabaret, and Tuesday is karaoke. (📞702-794-2300; www.freezonelv.com; 610 E Naples Dr; ⏱24hr; 🚌108)

Entertainment

Joint
LIVE PERFORMANCE

 14 Map p82, C6

Concerts at the Hard Rock's scaled-down music venue, holding just 4000 people, feel like private shows, even when rock royalty like the Red Hot Chili Peppers are in town. Intimate acoustic shows happen inside Vinyl lounge (cover charge varies, from nothing up to $40), off the main casino floor. (📞702-693-5222; www.hardrockhotel.com; Hard Rock; most tickets $40-200; 🚌108)

Shopping

Inyo Fine Cannabis Dispensary
DISPENSARY

 15 Map p82, E2

One of the first medical marijuana dispensaries in Las Vegas is all set for the burgeoning legal recreational market. (📞702-707-8888; www.inyolasvegas.com; 2520 Maryland Pkwy #2; ⏱10am-8pm)

Commercial Center
SHOPPING CENTER

 16 Map p82, D1

A local institution, this vast and somewhat seedy strip mall is endlessly fascinating, revealing life beyond the Strip. Occupants include two gay saunas, a swingers' joint, a wig shop and various cheap and tasty ethnic restaurants. (📞702-737-3478; www.commercialcenterdistrict.com; 953 E Sahara Ave; ⏱hours vary)

Understand
The Fruit Loop

LGBT visitors always ask, 'Where's the gay Strip?' and the answer is always, 'There isn't one,' save for what has been brazenly nicknamed the 'Fruit Loop,' a section of Paradise Rd south of Harmon Ave between Hard Rock casino and the University of Nevada Las Vegas (UNLV), about a mile east of the Strip. There's a gay-centric weighting among the dozen or so bars and clubs comprising its growing-in-fits-and-spurts LGBT scene, although a mixed clientele is generally welcomed everywhere, and some haunts do have girls' nights for girls only.

Explore

West of the Strip

Why bother heading west of the Strip, you might ask, where the cookie-cutter suburbs rolling onto the Spring Mountains are only interrupted by a casino or three and a dozen strip joints. Well, how about a sky-high zipline, Vegas' newest casino, an eco-minded desert oasis and the bustling Chinatown Plaza and suddenly you've got plenty of reasons to head west.

The Sights in a Day

☀ Start the day by flying 400ft in the air between the Rio's two hotel towers on the **VooDoo Zipline** (p94), then settle your stomach at the resort's **Carnival World Buffet** (p96), still one of the best in town. Spend the rest of the morning exploring Nevada's natural history at the family-friendly **Springs Preserve** (p90), featuring interactive exhibits, the eco-friendly Desert Living Center, a stalactite cave and the massive state fossil, part of the newly relocated **Nevada State Museum** (p91). Finish with a stroll around the preserve's lovely desert gardens.

☀ For a break from the inflated prices and flashy restaurants on the Strip, head to **Chinatown Plaza** (p96) for late lunch. Hong Kong barbecue houses, Vietnamese pho shops, Japanese sushi bars and pan-Asian bubble-tea dispensaries cluster around the telltale Chinese gate.

☾ The most glamorous attraction west of the Strip is the soaring **Palms** (p94) casino-resort. Feast on steak at the dramatically lit **N9NE** (p96) before kicking back with cocktails at **Ghostbar** (p96), or crossing over to the Rio for drinks on the terrace at **VooDoo Rooftop Nightclub** (p97).

 Top Sights

Springs Preserve (p90)

💜 **Best of Las Vegas**

Off-Strip Dining

Chinatown Plaza (p96)

Ping Pang Pong (p96)

Raku (p91)

Live Entertainment

Penn & Teller (p97)

For Kids

Springs Preserve (p90)

Getting There

🚌 **Bus** Run east–west and north–south on major streets, including Tropicana Ave (bus 201), Flamingo Rd (202) and through Chinatown on Spring Mountain Rd (203).

Shuttle Free shuttles run between Rio and Harrah's and Bally's/Paris Las Vegas on the Strip and between the Orleans and Gold Coast casinos.

🚕 **Taxi** One-way fares to the Strip average $10 to $20, to Downtown $20 to $25 (plus tips).

Top Sights
Springs Preserve

When you just need to get some fresh air and get off the Strip, but don't want to travel too far, Springs Preserve is your best bet. It's situated on the site where now-dry natural springs once fed *las vegas* (Spanish for 'the meadows'), and southern Paiutes and Old Spanish Trail traders set up camp. It's a literal oasis in the desert and one of Vegas' truly kid-friendly attractions.

👁 Map p92, B1

📞 702-822-7700

www.springspreserve.org

333 S Valley View Blvd

adult/child $19/11

🕘 9am-5pm

♿; 🚌104

Garden

Origen Museum

Visitors who want to dig beneath the surface of this desert oasis should start at the Origen Museum. The Natural Mojave gallery simulates flash floods and shows the wildlife of the desert. The 'People of the Springs' exhibit narrates Las Vegas' history, from Native American dwellings to the construction of the railroad and the Hoover Dam. The New Frontier rooms are full of interactive games and kid-friendly activities about conservation, the environment and life in the modern-day city.

Desert Living Center

Nevada's first platinum-certified LEED (Leadership in Energy and Environmental Design) buildings have been constructed from recycled materials and with rammed-earth walls, with passive cooling, renewable heating, reclaimed water and solar-electricity panels, all harvesting clean energy and exemplifying the green future of sustainable design. Inside are classrooms, learning labs and family oriented exhibits such as the 'Compost Crawl' and 'Garbage Truck Theater.'

Nevada State Museum

Inside the state's natural and cultural history **museum** (☎702-486-5205; http://nvdtca.org/museums; 309 S Valley View Blvd; adult/child $20/12; ☺9am-5pm Tue-Sun; ♿), explore more educational exhibits including prehistoric skeletons such as Nevada's state fossil (the ichthyosaur *Shonisaurus popularis*), a replica of a stalactite cave, an atomic explosion display and exhibits covering Sin City's glamorous bygone days.

Gardens & Trails

Almost 4 miles of nature trails are signposted with interpretive displays piecing together Nevada's legacy, from Native Americans to Western pioneers. Take a train ride or rent a bike on weekends to explore them.

☑ **Top Tips**

▶ Uber and Lyft ride-share services take the hassle and expense out of travel to and from the park.

▶ Plan your day. There are lots of great cheap eats not too far from the park, but decide where to go in advance to save time on the day and help keep those hungry kids happy.

▶ For an all-out nature day, combine a park visit with a half-day trip to Red Rock Canyon (best if you have your own wheels).

✕ **Take a Break**

Lovers of authentic Japanese food without the celebrity Strip treatment will want to round out the day with dinner at **Raku** (☎702-367-3511; www.raku-grill.com; 5030 W Spring Mountain Rd; shared plates $5-20; ☺6pm-3am Mon-Sat; ☐203), easily one of Las Vegas' best restaurants.

SYMPHONY PARK

Casino Center Blvd

Main St

DOWNTOWN

W Charleston Blvd

Grand Central Pkwy

Main St

W Wyoming Ave

S Las Vegas Blvd (The Strip)

E Sahara Ave

SLS

Karen Ave

Martin Luther King Blvd

Highland Dr

Western Ave

S Industrial Rd

W Sahara Ave

Mesquite Ave

Sunland Ave

Alta Dr

Shadow St

Tonopah Dr

Ellis St

Waldman Ave

Bannie Ave

Silver Ave

Pine St

Rancho Dr

S Rancho Dr

W Oakey Blvd

Rancho Dr

Circus Cir

Rancho Cir

Las Vegas Expwy

Rosemary La

Pinto La

Palomino La

Campbell Dr

Kenny Way

Lacy La

Ashby Ave

Calle de Espana

Merritt Ave

Springs Preserve

S Valley View Blvd

S Valley View Blvd

Rotary Park

Cragin Park

Hinson St

Las Verdes St

San Bernardino Ave

S Valley View Bl

Meadows La

Alta Dr

Lions Park

Bedford Rd

Arville St

W Charleston Blvd

Decatur Blvd

W Oakey Blvd

W Sahara Ave

S Decatur Bl

Westgate
Las Vegas

Las Vegas Convention Dr
Convention
Center

Sierra Vista Dr

Elm Dr

E Twain Ave

Paradise Rd

Paradise Rd

For reviews see

◆ Top Sights	p90
◉ Sights	p94
✕ Eating	p94
◉ Drinking	p96
✿ Entertainment	p97

Riviera Blvd

Convention Center Dr

Las Vegas Convention &
Visitors Authority

E Desert Inn Rd

Wynn
Golf Club

E Flamingo Rd

Harrah's/The LINQ

Flamingo/Caesars Palace

Bally's/Paris
Las Vegas

Rochelle Ave

Lana Ave

Koval La

0   1 km
0   0.5 miles

Sammy Davis Jr Dr

Highland Dr

Sands Ave

Treasure
Island

Audrie St

MGM
Grand

Westwood Dr

Mirage

THE STRIP

S Las Vegas Blvd (The Strip)

Rigel Ave

Dean Martin Dr

Bellagio

CityCenter

CITYCENTER

Monte
Carlo

Excalibur

W Tropicana Ave

Meade Ave

Sirius Ave

Polaris Ave

Polaris Ave

W Harmon Ave

Tompkins Ave

S Valley View Blvd

Procyon Ave

Rio

VooDoo
ZipLine

S Valley View Blvd

Wing St

Wynn Rd

Pioneer Ave

Schiff Dr

✕5 ✕6

S Valley View Blvd

Gold Coast

Palms

Rochelle Ave

Nevso Dr

Ave

Wynn Rd

Bell Dr

Arville St

Viking Rd

W Flamingo Rd

Arville St

Cameron St

W Desert Inn Rd

Twain Ave

W Rochelle Ave

W Harmon Ave

W Tropicana Ave

S Decatur Blvd

Fellwood Ave

5

6

7

8

A   B   C   D   E

Sights

VooDoo ZipLine ADVENTURE SPORTS

1 Map p92, C7

How does 'flying' between Rio's two towers sound? Strap into a seat on a 50-story tower. Four hundred feet below is the expansive pool area; beyond is the cityscape. Once the oper-ator sets you free, you'll whiz down 800ft of metal lines to a lower tower, then get pulled back! (📞702-388-0477; www.voodoo zipline.com; Rio; $27; ⏱11am-midnight)

Palms CASINO

2 Map p92, B7

The ultramodern Palms casino hotel burns brightly with a mix of entertainment designed to seduce gen-Xers and -Yers. Infamous for its starring role on MTV's *Real World: Las Vegas* series, the Palms has a high-drama, neon-lit feel that's equal parts sexy and sleazy. With some of the best odds near the Strip, the casino ropes in plenty of tourists and locals. (📞702-942-7770; www.palms.com; 4321 W Flamingo Rd; ⏱24hr; 🚌202)

Rio CASINO

3 Map p92, B7

Despite its giddy Carnaval theme, the all-suites Rio casino hotel is often overshadowed by the action at the Palms across the street. Occupying most of its corny two-story 'Masquerade Village' is a 100,000-sq-ft casino decked out with a colorful motif and more than 1200 slot machines, 80 table games, a full-service race and sports book with 100 TVs and a cut-throat poker room that's home to the **World Series of Poker** (www.wsop.com; Rio; ⏱May-Jul) finals. (📞866-746-7671; www.riolasvegas.com; 3700 W Flamingo Rd; ⏱24hr; 🚌free Strip shuttle)

Gold Coast CASINO

4 Map p92, B7

The neighborhood west of the Strip has several old-school casino hotels, such as Gold Coast – now as well known for its authentic Chinese cuisine as its gaming tables and slot machines that target locals, retirees and the package-tour crowd. (📞702-367-7111; www.goldcoastcasi-no.com; 4000 W Flamingo Rd; ⏱24hr; 🚌202)

Eating

Veggie Delight VEGETARIAN $

5 Map p92, B6

This Buddhist-owned, Vietnamese-flavored vegetarian and vegan kitchen makes chakra-color-coded tonics, *banh mi*-style sandwiches, hot pots and noodle soups. (📞702-310-6565; www.veggiedelight.biz; 3504 Wynn Rd; menu $3-10; ⏱11am-9pm Wed-Mon; 🍴)

Hot n Juicy Crawfish SEAFOOD $$

6 Map p92, B6

The name says it all: spicy, hot and juicy crawfish served by the pound or in baskets and a wide range of other seafood treats. Crazily popular. (📞702-891-8889; www.hotnjuicycrawfish.com; 4810 Spring Mountain Rd; baskets $12-20; ⏱noon-10pm Sun-Thu, to 11pm Fri & Sat; 🅿🍴♿)

Understand

Frontier Days

For many hundreds of years, Southern Paiute tribespeople lived a relatively peaceful if arduous existence in the desert around the present-day Las Vegas Valley. They were the descendants of Paiutes, one of the Native American tribes who lived near the Grand Canyon along the Colorado River. Their undoing as the dominant people of the region began with the arrival of Europeans.

Discovering the Springs

In 1829 Rafael Rivera, a scout for a Mexican trading expedition, was likely the first outsider to locate the natural springs in this valley, which Spanish colonists called *las vegas* ('the meadows'). Another traveler along the Old Spanish Trail, US Army officer John C Fremont, arrived in 1844 to explore and map the area. (Las Vegas' main downtown artery, Fremont St, bears his name today.)

The Mormon 'Invasion'

Amid the legions of miners who arrived later in the mid-19th century was a group hell-bent on doing God's work. These Mormons were sent from Salt Lake City by church leader Brigham Young to colonize the state of Deseret, their spiritual homeland. In 1855 the Mormons built a fort near what is now downtown Las Vegas, but abandoned it less than two years later. After the US Civil War (1861–65), small farms and ranches flourished in the Las Vegas Valley.

Arrival of the Railroad

On January 30, 1905, a railroad linking Salt Lake City with Los Angeles was completed in southern Nevada at a place called Jean, only 25 miles from Las Vegas. Later that year, during two days in mid-May, pioneers and real-estate speculators from LA bid for land in the newly established Las Vegas townsite, with some lots being auctioned off for up to 10 times their original asking price.

Ping Pang Pong
CHINESE $$

Asian package tourists and Chinatown locals vote with their feet, and it's always crowded here (see 4 Map p92, B7). Designed by chef Kevin Wu, a wok-tossed menu ranges from Beijing seafood stew to Shanghai noodles to Cantonese sausage fried rice. The dim sum carts roll until 3pm daily. (☏702-367-7111; www.goldcoastcasino.com; 4000 W Flamingo Rd, Gold Coast; mains $10-24; ⏱10am-3pm & 5pm-3am; ☒202)

Alizé
FRENCH $$$

Las Vegas chef André Rochat's top-drawer gourmet room (see 2 ◉ Map p92, B7) is named after a gentle Mediterranean trade wind. Enjoyed by nearly every table, panoramic floor-to-ceiling views of the glittering Strip are even more stunning than the haute French cuisine and remarkably deep wine cellar. Reservations essential; upscale dress code. (☏702-951-7000; www.alizelv.com; 4321 W Flamingo Rd, Palms; mains $46-68, tasting menu without/with wine pairings $155/245; ⏱6-10pm; ☒202)

N9NE
STEAK $$$

The Palms' dramatically lit steakhouse (see 2 ◉ Map p92, B7) lets A-list celebs lounge inside a semiprivate curtained dining space in the middle of a see-and-be-seen dining room. The beautifully aged steaks and chops keep on coming, along with everything from oysters Rockefeller to mushrooms stuffed with king crab and Gruyère cheese. Reservations essential; dress to impress. (☏702-933-9900; www.palms.com; 4321 W Flamingo Rd, Palms; mains $23-72; ⏱5:30-10pm Sun-Thu, to 11pm Fri & Sat; ☒202)

Carnival World Buffet
BUFFET $$$

Las Vegas' largest all-around buffet (see 3 ◉ Map p92, B7) is found at Rio (p94), with stir-fries, pizza, a taco bar and house-made gelato. There's a seafood add-on for those who can't get enough snow crab legs, lobster tails and freshly shucked oysters. (☏702-777-7757; www.riolasvegas.com; Rio; per person $25-45; ⏱11am-10pm; ♿; ☒free Strip shuttle)

☑ Top Tip

Chinatown Las Vegas

West from the Strip, along Spring Mountain Rd, is the heart of Vegas' strip-mall Chinatown. Slightly off the tourist radar, **Chinatown Plaza** (Map p92, B6; ☏702-221-8448; 4255 Spring Mountain Rd; most mains $6-18; ⏱hours vary; ♿; ☒203) is a favorite with local foodies for its late-night Vietnamese noodle shops, Japanese sushi bars, Korean barbecue grills and more. Start at the eye-catching Chinese gate.

Drinking

Ghostbar
LOUNGE

A clubby crowd, often thick with pop-culture celebs and pro athletes, packs the Palms' (p94) sky-high watering hole (see 2 ◉ Map p92, B7). DJs spin hip-hop and house while wannabe gangsters and Jersey girls sip pricey cocktails. The plush mansion decor and 360-degree panoramas are to die for. Dress to kill. Happy hour goes until 10pm nightly. (📞702-942-6832; www.palms.com; 4321 W Flamingo Rd, Palms; cover $10-25; ☺8pm-4am; 🚇202)

VooDoo Rooftop Nightclub
CLUB

The distant views of the Strip's neon glow from the outdoor patio are fantastic, but the DayGlo decor and DJs inside VooDoo (see 3 ◉ Map p92, B7) are just for laughs. An unpretentious crowd dances to old-school, retro and techno tunes while swigging exotic, oversized cocktails steaming with dry ice. Retirees and buttoned-down conventioneers let loose here. (📞702-777-6875; www.riolasvegas.com; Rio; cover $20-30; ☺8pm-2am Sun-Thu, to 3am Fri & Sat; 🚇free Strip shuttle)

Entertainment

Penn & Teller
COMEDY

Rio's (p94) star performers (see 3 ◉ Map p92, B7), this odd couple (one talks, the other doesn't) has been creating and destroying illusions for more than two decades, with dry wit, peppery profanity and some amazing stunts such as catching bullets in their teeth. The gimmick? They explain some (but not all) of their tricks to the audi-

---

---

ence. Stick around after the show for autographs and selfies. (📞702-777-2782; www.pennandteller.com; Rio; tickets from $89; ☺9pm Sat-Wed; 🚇free Strip shuttle)

Pearl
THEATER

A shining beacon for pop divas and rock bands, the Palms' (p94) 2500-seat concert hall (see 2 ◉ Map p92, B7) has a sophisticated sound system. Comedy kingpins and modern rockers from Gwen Stefani to Morrissey have burned up this stage, with most seats only 120ft or less away from the performers. Live albums are minted at the state-of-the-art recording studio. (📞702-944-3200; www.palms.com; 4321 W Flamingo Rd, Palms; most tickets $50-100; 🚇202)

Explore

Downtown & Fremont Street

With the retro casinos of the Fremont Street Experience, the vibrant Arts and Fremont East Entertainment Districts, cheap digs, cool museums and free entertainment galore, a visit or stay in massively rejuvenated Downtown is definitely an antidote for all Strip-related maladies.

The Sights in a Day

☀ Pop into the **Mob Museum** (p102) for an overview of organized crime in America from the turn of the 20th century to the present. Head west on Stewart Ave to elegant **Main Street Station** (p111) for a self-guided tour of the eclectic antiques collection and a taste of the house microbrew at **Triple 7** (p114).

☀ Walk east through the heart of Glitter Gulch, where Vegas' original Strip has been refashioned into the Fremont Street Experience. Step into the classy **Golden Nugget** (p100) to ogle the gigantic Hand of Faith and the 200,000-gallon shark tank. Continue east into the Fremont East Entertainment District to pick up hip threads and accessories at **Container Park** (p105). As the sun goes down, the bars around here come to life.

☾ When the moon is high in the sky, admire the glow of vintage neon signs at the outdoor **Neon Museum** (p109), including Aladdin's Lamp (from the now-demolished Aladdin Hotel on the Strip). Walk toward the glowing neon sign in the shape of a martini glass, then stop into **Downtown Cocktail Room** (p114) for Prohibition-era cocktails.

For a local's day in Fremont Street, see p104; for local life Downtown, see p106.

👁 Top Sights

Golden Nugget (p100)

Mob Museum (p102)

🔍 Local Life

Fremont Street East Food & Booze (p104)

Downtown Arts District (p106)

💜 Best of Las Vegas

Off-Strip Dining

Andiamo Steakhouse (p113)

Carson Kitchen (p105)

La Comida (p105)

eat. (p112)

Cocktail Bars

Downtown Cocktail Room (p114)

Beauty Bar (p105)

Shopping

Gamblers General Store (p115)

Rainbow Feather Dyeing Co (p107)

Williams Costume Company (p115)

Getting There

🚌 **Bus** Deuce & SDX head to and from the Strip.

🚕 **Taxi** $15 to $25 one way (plus tip) to or from the Strip.

Top Sights
Golden Nugget

Day or night, the Golden Nugget is Downtown's poshest address. With classy eateries and a swimming pool famous for its shark tank, it outshines the competition. This swank joint rakes in a moneyed crowd with a 38,000-sq-ft casino populated by table games and slot machines with the same odds as at Strip megaresorts. The nonsmoking poker room hosts daily tournaments.

Map p108, C2

702-385-7111

www.goldennugget.com

129 Fremont St E

24hr

P

Deuce, SDX

Shark Tank

Hand of Faith
The Golden Nugget's namesake claim to fame is the Hand of Faith. It's not a religious relic, but the heftiest hunk of gold ever found, weighing a massive 61lb 11oz (28kg). Discovered in Australia, it's now on display under glass near the North Tower elevators.

Shark Tank
Slip outside onto the pool terrace to gawk at the enormous shark tank – be sure to walk around to the back side for the best views. Yes, those are hotel guests hurtling through the aquarium: an innovative enclosed water slide spirals down three stories through the tank, providing a unique aquatic experience for thrill-seekers.

Casino
Check out the polished brass and white leather seats in the Golden Nugget's casino: day or night, this is Downtown's poshest address. The airy, nonsmoking poker room stages daily poker tournaments.

Chart House
If you dig the shark tank, get a load of the Golden Nugget's other creatively positioned aquarium. Vegas' branch of the high-end **Chart House** (☎702-386-8364; www.goldennugget.com/lasvegas; 129 Fremont St E, Golden Nugget; mains $19-45; ⊙11:30am-midnight Sun-Thu, to 1am Fri & Sat) chain eatery is anchored by a stunning 75,000-gallon aquarium and serves a variety of aquatic delights from Alaskan sea bass to coconut shrimp prepared practically any way you like.

☑ Top Tips
▶ For a closer look at the Shark Tank, take a behind-the-scenes tour ($30).

▶ For a peek at some smaller fry, stop for a drink at Chart House, a seafood restaurant where you can perch at the bar encircling a 75,000-gallon tropical aquarium.

✕ Take a Break
Nip around the corner and check out the expansive urban oasis that is Gold Spike (p106); with its playroom, living room and backyard, there's something for everyone.

Otherwise, for a sunny beverage and bar snacks, head to the northeast corner of Fremont and Las Vegas Blvd and grab a patio seat at Park on Fremont (p104).

Top Sights
Mob Museum

Opened to great fanfare on February 14, 2012 – the 83rd anniversary of the notorious St Valentine's Day Massacre in Chicago – this museum is officially known as the National Museum of Organized Crime & Law Enforcement. Even the museum's physical location is impressive, inside a historic US federal courthouse where mobsters sat for hearings in 1950–51.

👁 Map p108, D1

📞 702-229-2734

www.themobmuseum.org

300 Stewart Ave

adult/child $24/14

🕘 9am-9pm

P 🚌 Deuce

THE HEARINGS

Mob Museum Exhibits

With a board of directors headed up by a former FBI Special Agent, this museum takes its sensationalist subject seriously. Thoughtfully curated exhibits tell the story of organized crime in America from the perspective of both gangsters and coppers.As well as FBI equipment and mob-related artifacts, the museum boasts a series of multimedia exhibits featuring interviews with real-life Tony Sopranos.

Mob Museum Theater

Break up your journey through the museum's exhibits by plonking yourself down in a plush theater seat to watch videos projected on the big screen. If you're looking for History Channel–style documentaries, you'll be disappointed – most of the clips being shown are classic Hollywood gangster movies.

Gift Shop

The Mob Museum gift shop is a trove of offbeat Sin City souvenirs, whether you're on the hunt for a gangster fedora, a spy pen that writes with ultraviolet ink or a coffee mug with a handle made of brass knuckles. On a nerdy note, the shop fills its bookshelves with respectable tomes on the history of Sin City and the American Mafia.

Historic Architecture

Listed on the National Register of Historic Places, the building that houses the museum was built in 1933 and was once the Las Vegas post office and courthouse. It's one of the oldest buildings in Las Vegas, a city that only really got started as recently as 1905. On the proviso that it be restored and used for cultural purposes, the federal police, who operated the courthouse, sold the building in 2002 to the City of Las Vegas for the princely sum of $1!

☑ Top Tips

▶ The museum extends its educational mission by hosting special events, such as author readings and talks on everything from true-crime stories to casino cheating.

▶ Fascinating panel discussions take place inside the historic courtroom.

✘ Take a Break

Head down to nearby **Evel Pie** (☏702-840-6460; http://evelpie.com; 508 Fremont St E; pizza slices $4-5.50, whole pies $21-30; ◷11am-2am) for a slice of mobster-y pizza.

Directly opposite you'll find **Flippin' Good Burgers & Fries** (☏702-776-7991; http://flippingood.com; 505 Fremont St E; burgers $5-11; ◷11am-11pm Sun-Thu, to 2am Fri & Sat) where the burgers are... well, you know how this ends.

Local Life
Fremont Street East Food & Booze

The section of Fremont St east of Las Vegas Blvd and the few blocks south forms the Fremont East Entertainment District, aka 'Fremont East.' Like any good cocktail, it's a highly concentrated jolt of fun and flavor, chock-full of party haunts and drinking holes from dive bars to discos, and some of Vegas' most impressive (and chill), niche eateries.

1 **Park on Fremont**

Even if you're drunk already (not that we condone such unruly behavior), it's only a short stumble to the northern side of Fremont St E once you hop off the bus from the Strip. Here you'll find **Park on Fremont** (☎702-834-3160; www.parkonfremont.com; 506 Fremont St E; light meals $9-14; ⏰11am-3am), a fabulous little gastropub with sunny front and back patios perfect for people-watching and planning your next move.

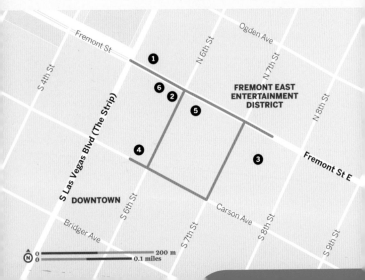

2 Commonwealth

It might be a little too cool for school, but **Commonwealth's** (📞702-445-6400; www.commonwealthlv.com; 525 Fremont St E; ⏱7pm-late Tue-Sat; 🚌Deuce) Prohibition-era interior is worth a look, featuring plush booths, softly glowing chandeliers, Victorian-era bric-a-brac and a saloon bar. Better still, imbibe your old-fashioned cocktails on the rooftop patio overlooking the Fremont East scene. They say there's a secret cocktail bar within the bar, but you didn't hear that from us.

3 Container Park

An incubator for up-and-coming fashion designers and local artisans by day, **Container Park** (📞702-359-9982; http://downtowncontainerpark.com; 707 Fremont St E; ⏱11am-9pm Mon-Thu, 10am-10pm Fri & Sat, to 8pm Sun) goes adults only (21-plus) after 9pm. When the sun sets, the container bars come to life and host regular themed events and movie nights. With food-truck-style menus, outdoor patio seating and late-night hours, food vendors inside the complex sell something to satisfy everyone's appetite.

4 Keep Your Brain Balanced

Health professionals recommend not drinking on an empty stomach, but you've probably already done that, so why not tidy yourself up and hit up **Carson Kitchen** (📞702-473-9523; www.carsonkitchen.com; 124 S 6th St; tapas & mains $8-22; ⏱11:30am-11pm Thu-Sat, to 10pm Sun-Wed; 🚌Deuce) for scrumptious share plates or **La Comida** (p112) for kickass Mexican with lashings of tequila.

5 Fremont Country Club

It's Vegas, so the night is young (whatever time it is) and there's usually always something going on at the **Fremont Country Club** (📞702-382-6601; www.fremontcountryclubvegas.com; 601 Fremont St E; ticket prices vary; ⏱show times vary), a sprawling old-school concert hall in the heart of Fremont East. Check the website for listings: expect anything from rock to alternative, blues to country, punk to pop.

6 Beauty Bar

If you're ready to kick on, keep it classy for **Beauty Bar** (📞702-598-3757; www.thebeautybar.com; 517 Fremont St E; cover free-$10; ⏱9pm-4am; 🚌Deuce), where you'll be swilling cocktails or chilling with the local glitterati inside the salvaged innards of a 1950s New Jersey beauty salon. DJs and live bands rotate nightly, spinning everything from tiki lounge tunes to disco, '80s hits to punk, as well as metal, glam and indie rock.

Local Life
Downtown Arts District

Making a masterpiece takes time, and Downtown's Arts District remains a work in progress: a hodgepodge of artist studios, compact galleries, quirky street art and storefronts – no wonder it's the epicenter of the monthly **First Friday** (p112) parties. It's also one of the few 'walk-friendly' spots in the city, despite retaining a gritty true-to-its-roots charm.

❶ Gold Spike
Gold Spike (☏702-476-1082; www.goldspike.com; 217 N Las Vegas Blvd; ⏰24hr), with its playroom, living room and backyard, is many things: bar, nightclub, performance space, work space; host of roller derbies, discos, live bands or dance parties; or just somewhere to soak up the sun with a relaxed crew and escape mainstream Vegas. If you love it like the locals do, you can even

spend the night in the **Oasis at Gold Spike** (☏702-768-9823; www.oasisatgold-spike.com; 217 N Las Vegas Blvd; r from $29; P❄❅).

② Street Art Central
The alleyway between S 1st St and S Casino Blvd, between Bonneville Ave and Charleston Ave, is home to plenty of good graffiti, although you'll find the entire Arts District and the area around Fremont East to be a veritable living gallery of street art, including entire buildings and stories-high works by some of the world's best street artists.

③ Boutiques & Burlesque
The Arts District (also known by locals as '18b,' as it was planned to be 18 blocks of art...nobody is sure how many it actually is) is full of original boutiques, vintage stores, pop-up shops and clearance outlets, and it's constantly changing. Check out **Buffalo Exchange** (p115) and **Rainbow Feather Dyeing Co** (p115) for inspiration before dropping in on the **Burlesque Hall of Fame** (p111).

④ Art Square & Art Factory
Side by side, **Art Square** (☏702-300-4337; www.artsquarelv.com; 1017 & 1025 S 1st St; ⊙office hours 11am-5pm Mon-Fri, gallery hours vary; 🚍Deuce, SDX) and the **Arts Factory** (☏702-383-9907; www.theartsfac-

tory.com; 107 E Charleston Blvd; ⊙9am-6pm; 🚍Deuce, SDX) form the undisputed hub of the Arts District. Once a block of derelict buildings and warehouses, this is now ground zero for **First Fridays** (p112), when thousands roam around the vibrant area on the first Friday evening of every month.

⑤ Queer Beers, Bunnies and Bric-a-Brac
It's Vegas, so any time is a good time for some bar hopping. After all this walking, shopping and chatting with the locals, you're bound to be thirsty. So what's your flavor? If you're LGBT friendly, pop in to **Bastille on 3rd** (☏702-385-9298; www.bastillelv.com; 1402 S 3rd St; ⊙10am-2am), Vegas' first gay bar; the **Velveteen Rabbit** (p113) for arty mixology; or **ReBAR** (p114) if you're a mad vintage fan.

⑥ Breakfast at Vickie's
End your day the local way with a meal at **Vickie's Diner** (☏702-444-4459; www.vickiesdiner.com; 1700 S Las Vegas Blvd; meals $6-18; ⊙24hr; 🚻), a no-frills, no-fuss old-school diner where you can get a cheap feed (burgers, subs, sandwiches) or a fry-up breakfast: it's remarkable that there's been a diner here for so long, although it has changed hands over the years.

Las Vegas Expwy

Mesquite Ave

S 9th St

S 8th N

Fremont St E

Carson Ave

S 11th St

S Maryland Pkwy

FREMONT EAST
ENTERTAINMENT
DISTRICT

Bridger Ave

Lewis Ave

Clark Ave

E Charleston Blvd

S Las Vegas Blvd

Ogden Ave

El Cortez

9 ⊚

13 ✕

S 10th St

S 9th St

E Bonneville Ave

S 8th St

Mob
Museum

Neon Museum –
Urban Gallery

N Las Vegas Blvd

2 ⊚

8 ⊚

Slotzilla

18 14
✕ ✕

S 7th St

S 6th St

Graceland
Wedding Chapel

E Charleston Blvd

Stewart Ave

5 ⊚ Binion's

N 4th St

Gambling Hall

Fremont St

15 ✕

S Las Vegas Blvd (The Strip)

Main Street
Station

10 ⊚

Main St

Golden Gate

4 ⊚

Plaza

6 ⊚

Fremont St

Golden Nugget

7 ⊚

Carson Ave

Bridger Ave

Lewis Ave

S 3rd St

Vegas
Weddings

11 ⊚

DOWNTOWN

Clark Ave

Garces Ave

Gass Ave

Casino Center Blvd

Hoover Ave

Grand Central Pkwy

Las Vegas Expwy

City Pkwy

S 1st St

Discovery
Children's
Museum

3 ⊚

Symphony
Park

19 ✪

Promenade Pl

Coolidge Ave

22 ⊚

Main St

21 ⊚

17 20
⊚ ⊚

23 ⊚

16 ⊚

W Bonneville Ave

Burlesque
Hall of Fame

7 ⊚

Grand Central Pkwy

P

W Charleston Blvd

500 m
0.25 miles

N

Martin Luther King Blvd

For reviews see

⊚ Top Sights   p100
⊚ Sights   p109
✕ Eating   p112
⊚ Drinking   p113
✪ Entertainment   p114
⊡ Shopping   p115

Riviera sign, Neon Museum – Neon Boneyard

Sights

Neon Museum – Neon Boneyard   MUSEUM

1 ⊙ Map p108, E1

This nonprofit project is doing what almost no one else does: saving Las Vegas' history. Book ahead for a fascinating guided walking tour of the 'Neon Boneyard,' where irreplaceable vintage neon signs – Las Vegas' original art form – spend their retirement. Start exploring at the visitor center inside the salvaged La Concha Motel lobby, a mid-century modern icon designed by African American architect Paul Revere Williams. Tours are usually given throughout the day, but are most spectacular at night. (☎702-387-6366; www.neonmuseum.org; 770 N Las Vegas Blvd; 1hr tour adult/child $19/15, after dark $26/22; ⊙tours daily, schedules vary; ☐113)

Neon Museum – Urban Gallery   TOURS

2 ⊙ Map p108, D2

Plaques tell the story of each restored vintage neon sign at these open-air galleries. Look for the flashy 40ft-tall cowboy on horseback, Aladdin's sparkling genie lamp, a glowing martini glass, a flaming steakhouse sign and more. The biggest assemblages are inside the Neonopolis and on the 3rd St cul-de-sac just north of the

Fremont Street Experience (📞702-387-6366; www.neonmuseum.org; 450 Fremont St E, Neonopolis; admission free; ⏰24hr; 🚌Deuce, SDX)

Discovery Children's Museum

MUSEUM

3 ◉ Map p108, B2

Designed for toddlers to pre-teens, the Discovery Children's Museum has undergone a major overhaul and reopened in a state-of-the-art building in Symphony Park. Highlights include 'The Summit,' a 12-story tower of interactive activities and play space, plus themed educational and entertaining exhibits such as Eco City, Water World, Toddler Town, Fantasy Festival, Patents Pending and Young at Art. (📞702-382-3445; www.discoverykidslv.org; 360 Promenade Pl, Symphony Park; $14.50; ⏰10am-5pm Mon-Sat, noon-5pm Sun Jun-early Sep, 9am-4pm Tue-Fri, noon-5pm Sat & Sun rest of year; ♿; 🚌SDX)

Golden Gate

CASINO

4 ◉ Map p108, C1

A gambling hall and hotel have stood on this corner since 1906, one year after the whistle-stop railway town of Las Vegas was founded. It didn't become the Golden Gate until 1955, when a troupe of Italian Americans from San Francisco decamped and stayed on for four decades to manage what was previously known as the 'Sal Sagev' (the city's name spelled backwards). Today, the Golden Gate's hypnotic sign is almost as irresistible

as its famous shrimp cocktails. (📞702-385-1906; www.goldengatecasino.com; 1 Fremont St; ⏰24hr; 🚌Deuce, SDX)

Binion's Gambling Hall

CASINO

5 ◉ Map p108, D1

Binion's Gambling Hall was opened in 1951 (then known as Binion's Horseshoe), by notorious Texan gambler Benny Binion, who wore gold coins for buttons on his cowboy shirts and spurred the transformation of Fremont St casino hotels from sawdust gambling halls to classy carpet joints. Benny was among the first to offer free drinks for slot-machine players and airport limo rides for high rollers. Today, what appeals most about this bedraggled Downtown property is its genuine country-and-western flavor. (📞702-382-1600; www.binions.com; 128 Fremont St E; ⏰24hr; 🚌Deuce, SDX)

Plaza

CASINO HOTEL

6 ◉ Map p108, C1

Built on the site of a Union Pacific Railroad Depot, the Plaza opened in 1971. For decades it was a gaudy, cheap-looking hotel attracting package tourists and blue-haired, bingo-playing grandmothers. Although recently renovated with a fresher, more contemporary appearance, the place is far from pretentious – it still packs in loyal gamblers with its rowdy $5 blackjack tables and cocktail waiters who call you 'hun.' (📞702-386-2110; www.plazahotelcasino.com; 1 S Main St; ⏰24hr; 🚌Deuce, SDX)

Burlesque Hall of Fame   MUSEUM

7 Map p108, B4

Housed in the Art Square (p107) complex, this sweet museum pays homage to the history of burlesque performance in the USA. Gawk at fab sequined outfits and photographs of some of the genre's sultriest stars from yesteryear. (☎888-661-6465; www.burlesquehall.com; 1017 S 1st St #195; suggested donation $5; ⏰10am-6pm Tue-Sun; 🚌Deuce)

Slotzilla   ADVENTURE SPORTS

8 Map p108, D2

Soar through the air on ziplines strung underneath the Fremont Street Experience canopy from Slotzilla, a 12-story, slot-machine-themed platform with 35ft-tall showgirls. (www.vegasexperience.com/slotzilla-zip-line; Fremont St Mall, Fremont Street Experience; lower line $25, upper line $45; ⏰1pm-1am Sun-Thu, to 2am Fri & Sat; 👶; 🚌Deuce, SDX)

El Cortez   CASINO

9 Map p108, E2

Head to the unabashedly retro El Cortez, Vegas' oldest continuously operating casino, on the National Register of Historic Places. Going strong since 1941, it's one of the only carpet joints left where the slot machines are the real thing. If you hit the jackpot, you'll enjoy the clatter of actual coins – none of that newfangled paper ticket nonsense. (☎702-385-5200; www.

elcortezhotelcasino.com; 600 Fremont St E; ⏰24hr; 🚌Deuce)

Main Street Station   CASINO

10 Map p108, C1

This filigreed casino recreates Victorian opulence with its unique design, detailed craftwork and an extensive antiques collection. Pick up a brochure at the hotel's front desk and take a self-guided tour of the *objets d'histoires*. Highlights include exquisite bronze chandeliers (originally from an 1890s Coca-Cola building in Austin, TX), a graffiti-covered chunk of the Berlin Wall (now supporting a urinal in the men's restroom) and an art-nouveau chandelier from Paris' Figaro Opera House. (☎702-387-1896; www.mainstreetcasino.com; 200 N Main St; ⏰24hr; 🚌SDX)

 Top Tip

Fremont Street Experience

Streaking down the center of Vegas' Glitter Gulch historical district Downtown, **Fremont Street Experience** (☎702-678-5600; www.vegasexperience.com; Fremont St Mall; admission free; ⏰shows hourly dusk-midnight or 1am; 🚌Deuce, SDX) is a five-block pedestrian mall lined with old-school casinos and topped by an arched steel canopy. Hourly from dusk until midnight, the 1400ft-long canopy turns on an amiably cheesy six-minute light-and-sound show.

First Fridays

On the first Friday evening of each month, Downtown comes to life as art lovers, hipsters, foodies and musicians come out to play in the 18b Arts District and Fremont East Entertainment District. **First Friday** (www.ffflv.org; ⊘1st Friday every month 5-11pm) is like a giant block party, featuring art gallery openings, live music, performance art, children's activities and food trucks selling everything from snow cones to fried pickles.

Vegas Weddings
CEREMONY

11 ◉ Map p108, C3

With the only walk-up (and drive-thru) wedding window in Vegas, plus a cathedral-style chapel, this newly built place also arranges weddings at scenic outdoor spots such as **Valley of Fire** (🖉702-397-2088; www.parks.nv.gov/parks/valley-of-fire; 29450 Valley of Fire Hwy, Overton; per vehicle $10; ⊘visitor center 8:30am-4:30pm, park 7am-7pm), Lake Mead (p120) and the Grand Canyon (p116; 🖉702-933-3464; www.702wedding.com; 555 S 3rd St; drive-thru weddings from $99; ⊘7am-10:30pm Mon-Thu, 8am-midnight Fri & Sat, from 9am Sun)

Graceland Wedding Chapel
CHAPEL

12 ◉ Map p108, D3

Offering the original Elvis impersonator wedding (from $199) for over 50

years. If it's good enough for rock stars, then it's probably good enough for you, too. (🖉702-382-0091; www.gracelandchapel.com; 619 S Las Vegas Blvd; ⊘9am-11pm)

Eating

eat.
BREAKFAST $

13 🍴 Map p108, E2

Community spirit and creative cooking provide reason enough to venture off Fremont St to find this cafe. With a concrete floor and spare decor, it can get loud as folks chow down on truffled egg sandwiches, cinnamon biscuits with strawberry compote, shrimp po'boy sandwiches and bowls of New Mexican green-chili chicken *posole*. (🖉702-534-1515; http://eatdtlv.com; 707 Carson Ave; mains $7-14; ⊘8am-3pm Mon-Fri, to 2pm Sat & Sun; 🖉)

La Comida
MEXICAN $$

14 🍴 Map p108, D2

Meaning 'family meal,' La Comida's emphasis is on simple, culturally authentic dishes (soups, salads, tacos, enchiladas), presented in a warm, convivial environment to be shared with family. Why not throw some tequila into the mix (the restaurant has more varieties than it does seats), straight up or in sweet and salty margaritas, and get your Downtown evening started right? (🖉702-463-9900; www.lacomidalv.com; 100 6th St; mains $13-22; ⊘noon-10:30pm Tue-Thu, to midnight Fri & Sat, to 11pm Sun)

Graceland Wedding Chapel

Andiamo Steakhouse STEAK $$$

15  Map p108, D2

Of all the old-school steakhouses inside Downtown's carpet joints, the current front-runner is Joe Vicari's Andiamo Steakhouse. Upstairs from the casino, richly upholstered half-moon booths and impeccably polite waiters set the tone for a classic Italian steakhouse feast of surf-and-turf platters and housemade pasta, followed by a rolling dessert cart. Extensive Californian and European wine list. Reservations recommended. (☎702-388-2220; www.thed.com; 301 Fremont St E, The D; mains $24-79; ☺5-11pm; ☐Deuce, SDX)

Drinking

Velveteen Rabbit COCKTAIL BAR

16 Map p108, B4

Las Vegas wasn't always a shining neon star of craft cocktailery, but a new breed of lounges like Velveteen Rabbit have put the city on the mixology map. Located in the funky Arts District, it's a lively warren of artsy decor and inventive adult drinks. The beer program is laudable, too. (☎702-685-9645; http://velveteenrabbitlv.com; 1218 S Main St; ☺5pm-2am Mon-Sat, 7pm-1am Sun)

ReBAR

BAR

17 Map p108, B4

Las Vegas definitely revels in kitsch, and it absolutely loves drinking spots. ReBAR unites both. Located in the Arts District, it's a temple of nutty craft items, vintage bar signs, outrageous beer steins and one-of-a-kind doohickeys. Peruse the walls for that perfect retro souvenir, then sit down for a respectable selection of beers and spirits. Bask in the vintage glow. (☑702-349-2283; http://rebarlv.com; 1225 S Main St; ⏱4pm-midnight Tue-Thu, to 2am Fri & Sat)

Downtown Cocktail Room

LOUNGE

18 🚇 Map p108, D2

With a serious list of classic cocktails and housemade inventions, this low-lit speakeasy is undeniably romantic, and it feels decades ahead of Downtown's old-school casinos. The entrance is ingeniously disguised: the door looks like just another part of the wall until you discover the sweet spot you have to push to get in. Happy hour runs 4pm to 8pm weekdays. (☑702-880-3696; www.downtowncocktailroom.com; 111 S Las Vegas Blvd; ⏱4pm-2am Mon-Fri, 7pm-2am Sat; 🚌Deuce)

Triple 7

MICROBREWERY

This easygoing microbrewery (see 10 ◎ Map p108, C1) inside Main Street Station's casino (p111) pours samplers of its craft beers, particularly hoppy IPAs, as well as red, amber and golden ales, smoky porter and fruity seasonal brews like blueberry wheat beer or dark cherry stout. Happy hour runs 3pm to 6pm weekdays. (☑702-387-1896; www.mainstreetcasino.com; 200 N Main St, Main Street Station; ⏱11am-7am; 🚌SDX)

Entertainment

Smith Center for the Performing Arts

PERFORMING ARTS

19 ⭐ Map p108, B2

Brilliant acoustics and art-deco-inspired design are just part of the wow factor at this Downtown performing arts complex. It's also sustainably built, making it the first performing arts center of its size to achieve Silver Leadership in Energy and Environmental Design (LEED) status. Cabaret jazz, Broadway shows, classical and contemporary music, dance troupes and comedians are all part of the offerings. (☎702-749-2000; www.thesmithcenter. com; 361 Symphony Park Ave, Symphony Park; tickets from $20; ⊙schedule varies; ☒SDX)

Shopping

Buffalo Exchange CLOTHING

20 🔒 Map p108, B4

Trade in your nearly new garb for cash or credit at this savvy secondhand clothing chain dealing in 1950s to '90s vintage fashions, clubwear, costume goodies and designer duds. (www.buffalo exchange.com; 1209 S Main St; ⊙11am-8pm Mon-Sat, 11am-7pm Sun; ☒109, 202)

Williams Costume Company CLOTHING

21 🔒 Map p108, B4

Friendly staff have supplied the Strip's aspiring starlets with DIY costuming goods since 1957. Check out the head shots in the dressing rooms, then pick up some rhinestones, sequins, feathers etc. Rentals are ideal for Halloween masquerades, wacky themed weddings or partying anytime on the Strip.

(☎866-330-9824; www.williamscostumeco. net; 1226 S 3rd St; ⊙10am-5pm Mon-Sat; ☒Deuce)

Gamblers General Store GIFTS & SOUVENIRS

22 🔒 Map p108, B3

This authentic gaming supply superstore has it all, starting with one of Nevada's largest inventories of vintage and new slot machines, as well as full-size roulette, poker, craps and blackjack tables. Less expensive gambling paraphernalia makes for perfect Sin City souvenirs, including customizable poker chips, rainbow-colored dice and collectible decks of cards actually used in Vegas casinos. (☎702-382-9903; www. gamblersgeneralstore.com; 800 S Main St; ⊙9am-5pm; ☒108, Deuce)

Rainbow Feather Dyeing Co GIFTS & SOUVENIRS

23 🔒 Map p108, B4

Where to satisfy that boa fetish? Need turkey, chicken, duck, goose, pheasant, ostrich or peacock quills? Rainbow stocks a positively fabulous selection of fine feathers and fans for Vegas showgirl costumes in every possible hue, from fire-engine red and hot pink to neon green and jet black. (☎702-598-0988; www.rainbowfeatherco.com; 1036 S Main St; ⊙9am-4pm Mon-Fri, to 1pm Sat; ☒108, Deuce)

Top Sights
Grand Canyon

Getting There

🚗 The Grand Canyon is located 275 miles east of Las Vegas; a five-hour drive.

✈ On a tour with Papillon Grand Canyon Helicopters from the Strip (p118).

The Grand Canyon is the USA's best-known natural attraction. Measuring more than 275 miles long and more than a mile deep, it's an incredible spectacle of Technicolor rock strata. After initially being dismissed by Spanish conquistadors and Western pioneers as little more than an obstacle to exploration, in the late 19th century the canyon drew miners bent on exploiting its natural resources. Later, tourists arrived, seeking a romanticized wilderness ideal. When President Theodore Roosevelt visited in 1903, he sagely remarked, 'you cannot improve on it.'

Sweeping Vistas

Carved by the Colorado River, the canyon's peaks, buttes and rims give access to fantastic vistas. Descending into its depths on hiking and mule-riding trails reveals an amazing variety of landscape, wildlife and climates. For panoramic views of the canyon's geological layer cake, head over to Yavapai Observation Station (p119).

Driving along the Canyon's South Rim

The canyon rim is paralleled on the south side by a 33-mile paved scenic drive. The canyon dips in and out of view as the road passes through the piñon-juniper and ponderosa pine forests. Along these drives, pullouts offer jaw-dropping views, and interpretive signs explain the natural history, canyon features and geology.

Hermit Road Scenic Route follows the South Rim on the west side of Grand Canyon Village. Closed to private vehicles March to November, the road is serviced by the free park shuttle bus; cycling is encouraged because of the light traffic.

Desert View Drive is open to cars year round, starting east of Grand Canyon Village and following the canyon rim for 26 miles to Desert View, the park's eastern entrance.

Desert View Watchtower

Desert View Drive offers access to the 800-year old pueblo ruins behind the Tusayan Museum of Native American history and culture – not to mention the enchanting five-story-high **Desert View Watchtower** (www.nps.gov/grca; Desert View, East Enrance; ⏰8am-sunset mid-May–Aug, 9am-6pm Sep–mid-Oct, 9am-5pm mid-Oct–Feb, 8am-6pm Mar–mid-May), the highest point on the South Rim. Unparalleled views take in the canyon, the Colorado River, the San Francisco Peaks, the Navajo Reservation and the Painted Desert.

📞 928-638-7888

www.nps.gov/grca

20 South Entrance Rd

⏰ 7-day entry per car/individual $30/15

☑ Top Tips

▶ Open year-round, the South Rim is the most popular jumping-off point for exploring the park.

▶ Free park shuttles operate along three well-traveled routes.

▶ It's a 215-mile, five-hour drive between the South and North Rim visitor centers.

▶ Mule rides and rafting trips require advance planning.

✗ Take a Break

Grand Canyon Village is a convenient stopping point. After browsing the native crafts and local art on display in town, have cocktails on the back porch of the majestic El Tovar Hotel (p118). On the North Rim, try Grand Canyon Lodge Dining Room (p118).

Hiking Trails

South Rim hiking is a favorite, with options for every skill level. Beginning in Grand Canyon Village, the **Rim Trail** (www.nps.gov/grca; 🚶) is the most popular, and easiest. It connects scenic and historical sights over 13 miles.

The most popular of the corridor trails is scenic Bright Angel Trail. The steep 7.8-mile descent to the Colorado River is punctuated with four logical turnaround spots. Summer heat can be crippling; day hikers should either turn around at one of the resthouses (a 3- to 6-mile round-trip) or start at dawn.

The South Kaibab (South Rim) is one of the park's prettiest trails, combining stunning scenery and unobstructed, 360-degree views. During summer, rangers discourage all but the shortest day hikes along this steep, rough and exposed trail– otherwise it's a six-mile, grueling round trip. Turning around after 1.5 miles at Cedar Ridge makes a fine short day hike.

Horseback Riding in the Canyon

Due to erosion concerns, the National Park Service (NPS) no longer allows one-day mule rides down into the canyon. **Canyon Vistas Mule Rides** (📞888-297-2757, same day/next day reservations 928-638-3283; www.grandcanyonlodges. com; Bright Angel Lodge; 3hr ride $135, 1-/2-night ride incl meals & accom $552/788) offers a three-hour trip along a newly constructed four-mile trail beside the east rim or a two-day trip to the bottom of the canyon, which includes a night at Phantom Ranch.

Flying over the Canyon

Flights over the canyon have been restricted in number, altitude and routes to reduce noise pollution. Companies offering scenic helicopter and airplane flights include **Grand Canyon Airlines** (📞866-235-9422, 702-835-8484; www.grand canyonairlines.com) and **Papillon Grand Canyon Helicopters** (📞702-736-7243, 888-635-7272; www.papillon.com); routes and rates vary. Most flights leave from Tusayan or Las Vegas, but check itineraries carefully; Grand Canyon West isn't part of Grand Canyon National Park.

Grand Canyon Dining

At **Grand Canyon Lodge Dining Room** (📞May-Oct 928-638-2611, Nov-Apr 928-645-6865; www.grandcanyonforever.com; breakfast $8-11, lunch $10-13, dinner $18-28; ⏱6:30-10:30am, 11:30am-2:30pm & 4:30-9:30pm May 15-Oct 15; 🅿🚶) the windows are so huge that you can sit anywhere and enjoy good views over the North Rim. The menu includes regional treats such as western trout and buffalo flank steak. Reservations essential.

A stone's throw from the canyon's edge, **El Tovar** (📞928-638-2631; www. grandcanyonlodges.com; National Historic Landmark District; mains $20-30; ⏱restaurant 6-10:30am, 11am-2pm & 4:30-10pm, lounge 11am-11pm; 🚶; 🚍Village) has the best views of any restaurant in the state, if not the country. The grand stone-and-dark-oak dining room warms the soul like an upscale lodge of yore. Reservations are required for dinner. To avoid the lunchtime crowds, arrive before 11:45am.

Understand

Geology of the Grand Canyon

- -

The Grand Canyon captivates travelers because of its sheer immensity: it's a tableau that reveals the earth's history layer by dramatic layer. Mother Nature adds artistic details – rugged plateaus, crumbly spires, shadowed ridges – that flirt and catch your eye as the sun crosses the sky.

A River Runs Through It

Snaking along the canyon floor are 277 miles of the Colorado River, which has carved out the canyon during the past six million years and exposed rocks up to two billion years old – half the age of the earth. The sequences of rocks that make up the dramatic cliffs and plateaus, shaped by the river and the effects of wind erosion, include layers of limestone, sandstone, shale, granite and schist. At the **Yavapai Observation Station** (📞928-638-7888; ⏰8am-5pm, later in summer) on the South Rim, visitors can stroll along an interpretive trail that explains how these layers of rock were formed over time.

History Written on the Walls

Stand in the basin and look up: the Grand Canyon's towering walls are a mile high, offering a fascinating cross-section of the earth's crust. Forget millions of years – these walls represent two billion years of the earth's history. A guide can point out the crystalline rocks, likely the product of long-ago lava flows, in the trio of 'Granite Gorges.' Geologists estimate that these rocks metamorphosed around 1.75 billion years ago.

North Rim, South Rim

The two rims of the Grand Canyon offer quite different experiences; they lie more than 200 miles apart by road and are rarely visited on the same trip. Most visitors choose the South Rim for its easy access, wealth of services and vistas that don't disappoint. The quieter North Rim has its own charms: at 8200ft elevation (1000ft higher than the South Rim), its cooler temperatures support verdant meadows and tall, thick groves of trees. Head here for blessed solitude in nature's bounty – only 10% of park visitors make the trek. Meadows are thick with wildflowers and dense clusters of willowy aspen and spruce trees, the air is often crisp and the skies big and blue.

Top Sights
Hoover Dam & Lake Mead

Getting There

🚗 Hoover Dam is located 30 miles southeast of Las Vegas and is a 40-minute drive from the Strip.

Even those who question the USA's commitment to damming the US West have to marvel at the engineering and architecture of the Hoover Dam. Set amid the almost unbearably dry Mojave Desert, the dam towers over Black Canyon, the stretch of the Colorado River just below Hoover Dam, providing electricity for the entire region. Hoover Dam created Lake Mead, which boasts 700 miles of shoreline, while Davis Dam created the much smaller Lake Mohave, which straddles the Arizona border.

Lake Mead

Hoover Dam Tour

Guided tours of the architectural wonder begin at the visitor center. Take an elevator ride 50 stories below to view the dam's massive power generators, each of which alone could power a city of 100,000 people.

Boulder City/Hoover Dam Museum

You'll enjoy the dam tour more if you stop at the small but engagingly hands-on Hoover Dam Museum first. Exhibits focus on Depression-era America and the tough living conditions endured by the people who built the dam. A 20-minute film features historical footage of the project.

Mike O'Callaghan-Pat Tillman Memorial Bridge

Featuring a pedestrian walkway with perfect views upstream of Hoover Dam, the **Mike O'Callaghan-Pat Tillman Memorial Bridge** (Hwy 93) was named for Mike O'Callaghan, governor of Nevada from 1971 to 1979, and NFL star turned US Army Ranger Pat Tillman. Tillman, once a player for the Arizona Cardinals, was killed by friendly fire in Afghanistan in 2004.

Lake Mead National Recreational Area

It's less than an hour's drive from Las Vegas to the most visited northern section of the 1.5-million-acre **Lake Mead National Recreation Area** (☎info desk 702-293-8906, visitor center 702-293-8990; www.nps.gov/lake; Lakeshore Scenic Dr; 7-day entry per vehicle $10; ⏲24hr; ♿), a popular weekend camping destination for local residents. Within this protected area of the Mojave Desert are Lake Mead, which extends 110 miles toward the Grand Canyon; 67-mile-long Lake Mohave, which runs along the Arizona–Nevada border; and miles of spectacular desert around the lakes.

☎702-494-2517, 866-730-9097

www.usbr.gov/lc/hooverdam

off Hwy 93

admission visitor center incl parking $10

⏲9am-6pm Apr-Oct, to 5pm Nov-Mar

♿

☑ Top Tips

▶ At Hoover Dam, park for free on the other side of the Arizona state line and walk to the visitor center.

▶ Several companies on the Strip offer guided bus tours to Hoover Dam.

✗ Take a Break

Stop in Boulder City at a classic diner like the Coffee Cup (p122), or go for sandwiches and wine at lively Milo's Cellar (p122).

Water Sports on Lake Mead

Popular year-round activities on the lake include swimming, fishing, boating, water skiing and kayaking; **Vegas Watersports** (☑702-748-7873; www.las-vegaswatersports.net; 490 Horsepower Cove; ⏱6am-10pm) offers return transport from your hotel. A splendid scenic drive winds north along Lakeshore Dr and Northshore Rd, passing viewpoints, hiking and birding trailheads, beaches and bays, and full-service marinas.

Hiking from Lake to Dam

A 3.7-mile hiking trail along a historical railway line with five tunnels links Lake Mead's **Alan Bible Visitor Center** (☑702-293-8990; www.nps.gov/lake; Lakeshore Scenic Dr, off US Hwy 93; ⏱9am-4:30pm) to Hoover Dam. The most challenging hike in the park follows a 3-mile trail down 800ft to a set of hot springs in a slot off Black Canyon.

A Leisurely Lunchtime Cruise

Lake Mead Cruises (☑702-293-6180; www.lakemeadcruises.com; Lakeshore Rd; 90min cruise adult/child from $26/13; ⏱) offers kid-friendly tours, along with lunch and brunch cruises, on a triple-decker, air conditioned, Mississippi-style paddle wheeler. It departs from Hemenway Harbor.

Guided Adventures in the Desert

Let the outdoor experts show you the stunning landscape up close and personal. **Desert Adventures** (☑702-293-5026; www.kayaklasvegas.com; 1647a Nevada Hwy; full-day Colorado River kayak $179; ⏱9am-6pm Apr-Oct, 10am-4pm Nov-Mar) runs a range of half-, full- and multiday kayaking adventures on the Colorado River, as well as fishing, hiking and boating guided tours – including smooth water floats on the Colorado River through Black Canyon ($169). It also arranges multiday tours of the Grand Canyon and other outdoor tours.

Boulder City

On your way back to Las Vegas, stop for a stroll and a bite to eat in the relaxed but charming town of Boulder City, a rare casino-free town in Nevada. The town was originally erected to house workers constructing the Hoover Dam; today, it's a pleasant stop for travelers. Breakfast is served all day at the **Coffee Cup** (☑702-294-0517; www.worldfamouscoffeecup.com; 512 Nevada Way; mains $6-10; ⏱6am-2pm; ⏱), a downtown diner with a gourmet spin, while cozy **Milo's Cellar** (☑702-293-9540; www.milosbouldercity.com; 534 Nevada Hwy; mains $9-14; ⏱11am-10pm Sun-Thu, to 11pm Fri & Sat) serves wine and cheese in the evening.

Understand

History of Hoover Dam

A statue of bronze winged figures stands atop Hoover Dam, memorializing those who built the massive 726ft concrete structure – one of the world's tallest dams. The ambitious project resulted in a high number of human casualties, a fact many tourists don't realize as they're snapping pictures.

First Dam on the Colorado

Originally called Boulder Dam and later renamed after President Herbert Hoover, the Colorado River's first major dam was conceived as a New Deal public works project. Construction began in 1931, at the height of the Depression. Thousands of unemployed men – upwards of 10,000 and as many as 20,000 – arrived with their families, eager for work.

Tough Working Conditions

The settlement of Boulder City was planned to house workers, but accommodations weren't ready for the first wave; migrant families had to arrange their own housing. Conditions at the work site were bleak – desert temperatures soared to 120°F (49°C) and there were few available services in the area. The dam was the largest concrete structure of its kind to be built, and building efforts were characterized by risk, with some workers dangling hundreds of feet above the canyon. Sadly, hundreds lost their lives. But construction kept moving forward, the dam going up ahead of schedule and the new town of Boulder City growing. Casinos were outlawed there to prevent workers becoming distracted from their daytime task.

Glory Days

Hoover Dam was completed early, and under budget, in 1936. President Franklin D Roosevelt was present for the official dedication; afterwards, FDR continued on to Las Vegas – the first time a US president had paid a visit to Sin City. Several other famous figures – including Bette Davis and Howard Hughes – spent the night at the historic Boulder Dam Hotel after the dam was finished. Today, the historic hotel is the home of the Hoover Dam Museum. Confirming the dam's significance as a symbol of national pride, the landmark was closed to the public for the duration of WWII, and again in 1963 and 1969 after the respective deaths of Presidents Kennedy and Eisenhower.

The Best of
Las Vegas

Las Vegas' Best Walks

The Center Strip 126

Downtown 128

Las Vegas' Best...

Buffets 130

Architecture 131

Shopping 132

Nightlife 134

Casinos 136

Live Entertainment 138

Fine Dining 140

Local Culture 142

Off-Strip Dining 144

For Newlyweds 145

For Kids 146

Stardust sign, Neon Muesum – Neon Boneyard (p109)
IMAGE COURTESY OF THE NEON MUSEUM ©

Best Walks
The Center Strip

The Walk

The Strip is vast and vibrant, stretching for miles, but some of the most high-octane highlights and classic casino resorts conveniently flank a 1-mile section in the center. You'll hopscotch around Europe with stops in Paris, Venice, Lago di Como and ancient Rome, then get whisked on a side trip to tropical Polynesia. Dancing fountains, belching volcanoes, crooning gondoliers and a half-scale Eiffel Tower are all experiences likely to linger in your memory.

Start Paris Las Vegas

End Palazzo

Length 1.1 miles; two to four hours

Take a Break

Mojitos, caipirinhas and daiquiris are pure mixology magic at **Rhumbar** (📞702-792-7615; www.rhumbarlv.com; Mirage; 🕐noon-1am Sun-Wed, to 2am Thu-Sat, weather permitting), a Caribbean-flavored bar and cigar lounge at the Mirage.

VICTORIA DITKOVSKY/SHUTTERSTOCK ©

Fountain, Caesars Palace

❶ Paris Las Vegas

From the monorail station at the back of Bally's, sashay your way into **Paris Las Vegas** (p40) via the cobblestone shopping arcade Le Boulevard, soaking up *l'atmosphère* and stopping for croissants or crepes. Take a romantic ride up the **Eiffel Tower Experience** (p41) where you can view the **Fountains of Bellagio** (p23) from on high.

❷ Bellagio

Stay in a European mood by sauntering north to Flamingo Rd, then crossing Las Vegas Blvd on a skybridge to **Bellagio** (p22). Inside, admire glass flower sculptures and seasonal floral displays in the conservatory and designer fashions in the glamorous store windows of the Via Bellagio shopping promenade.

❸ Caesars Palace

Take the skybridge across Flamingo Rd and wander down to the plaza outside **Caesars Palace** (p54), where boozy lemonade is dispensed from the Spanish Steps. Inside this fantasia of classical antiquity, watch cocktail waiters dressed in togas parade underneath faux-frescoed ceilings. Meander through the vast **Forum Shops** (p72), then, exiting the mall by the grand spiral staircase, amble north along the Strip toward the tropical paradise of the Mirage.

❹ Mirage

Pause outside the **Mirage** (p57) to watch the faux volcano explode, then step inside the tropically scented hotel lobby to view the 20,000-gallon aquarium and the casino's domed rainforest atrium. If the tropics aren't your thing, channel 1960s London at Cirque du Soleil's show **Beatles LOVE** (p68) and the adjacent Revolution Lounge.

❺ Venetian

Wind down your walk on a graceful note by crossing the Strip toward the elegant **Venetian** (p44), with its flowing canals and mock-marble bridges. Treat yourself to a **gondola ride** (p45) with a singing gondolier or glide on your own

feet through the **Grand Canal Shoppes** (p46), then indulge in a well-deserved scoop of gelato at busy St Mark's Sq.

❻ Palazzo

Keep winding your way through the Grand Canal Shoppes into the **Palazzo** (p44), where a photo op in front of the indoor waterfall proves irresistible for many. To get back to where you started, catch the monorail at nearby Harrah's.

Best Walks
Downstown Downtown

🏃 The Walk

With the retro casinos of the Fremont Street Experience, vibrant hipster and art districts, affordable eats, cool museums and free entertainment galore, a stroll around Downtown is a great antidote to all that Strip glamour madness. You'll make the acquaintance of mobsters, marvel at a giant gold nugget, visit an edgy incubator for artists and designers, and be dazzled by vintage neon and a blazing sound-and-light after-dusk show.

Start Mob Museum

End Plaza

Length 0.9 miles; one to two hours

🍴 Take a Break

Make a pit stop in **Carson Kitchen** (p105), a tiny industrial-flavored eatery, to refuel on modern American share plates.

Golden Nugget

❶ Mob Museum

Take a stroll through Fremont St, stopping off in old-time casinos and hipster dive bars before visiting the thought-provoking **Mob Museum** (p102) for an overview of organized crime in the USA from the turn of the 20th century to the present.

❷ Main Street Station

Head west on Stewart Ave to **Main Street Station** (p111) for a self-guided tour of the eclectic antiques collection. Continue south on Main St past the rail car once owned by Wild West showman Buffalo Bill Cody.

❸ Fremont Street Experience

Walk east through the heart of Glitter Gulch, Vegas' original gambling quarter, reborn in 1995 as the **Fremont Street Experience** (p111). Adventure seekers whoosh overhead on the **Slotzilla** (p111) zipline, taking note of the unmissable modern-day neon icon Vegas Vickie.

4 Binion's Gambling Hall

Step inside historic **Binion's** (p110) to check out the action in the high-stakes poker room and watch real-life cowboys and cowgirls try their luck at blackjack.

5 Golden Nugget

Cross Fremont St to the classy **Golden Nugget** (p100). Ogle the gigantic Hand of Faith just off the casino floor, then slip out onto the pool terrace to gawk at the shark tank – the best views are from the back.

6 Neon Museum – Urban Gallery

Continue down to the **Neon Museum – Urban Gallery** (p109) and the alfresco assemblage of vintage neon signs installed on the 3rd St cul-de-sac just north of Fremont St.

7 Container Park

Keep going east toward the glowing neon martini glass welcoming you to the Fremont East Entertainment District, home to hipster watering holes such as **Commonwealth** (p105)

and the indie shops and eateries of the **Container Park** (p105).

8 Plaza

Head west back up Fremont St and wind up your walk at the revamped **Plaza** (p110), imagining what pioneer life was like when the adjacent former Union Pacific Railroad auctioned off dusty lots here in 1905. Head upstairs to Oscar's steakhouse and martini lounge for flight-deck views over the Fremont Street Experience.

Best
Buffets

The all-you-can-eat buffet is practically synonymous with Sin City: most major casino-hotels on the Strip offer impressive spreads every day, featuring live-action cooking stations where chefs in tall white hats prepare cuisines from around the world.

FITOPARDO.COM/GETTY IMAGES ©

Know your buffets

Weekend champagne brunch buffets, typically running from 10:30am to 3:30pm, are an especially hot ticket. Quality varies, so do your homework. Generally speaking, the more expensive the casino hotel, the better the food.

Veteran buffet-goers proffer a few words of advice. First, starve yourself for as long as possible, and don't count on eating any meals afterward. You'll get more for your money at breakfast or lunch – or, better yet, at the champagne brunch – than at dinner.

Best Buffets

Le Village Buffet Cooking stations from various French regions, fresh seafood and macaroons for dessert. (p62)

Wicked Spoon Buffet High-end feeding frenzy for cool kids with champagne option on weekends. (p61)

Buffet at Wynn Flower arrangements provide an elegant backdrop to this upscale food bonanza. (p62)

Bacchanal Live it up like the Romans did at the Strip's most lavish and expensive buffet. Baked-to-order soufflés, anyone? (p62)

Carnival World Buffet This oldie but goodie woos with housemade gelato and a seafood add-on option. (p96)

Spice Market Buffet A culinary carpet ride with stops in the Middle East, Asia, Mexico and Italy. (p64)

☑ **Top Tips**

▸ Show up early (eg before noon for Sunday brunch) to avoid the longest lines.

▸ Earn karma points by leaving a decent tip for the servers and busboys. Even though they're not taking your order, they have to clear an Everest's worth of dishes.

Buffet at Bellagio Not as swish as it once was, this spread is best for breakfast or lunch. (p64)

Cravings Though far from gourmet, this contender at the Mirage offers good value with its 11 cooking stations, IPAs on tap and luscious desserts. (p60)

Best
Architecture

In Vegas, there's the old and the new, the classic and the cutting-edge, the original and the copycat. As a general rule, you'll find the former Downtown and the latter – grandly, gaudily, quite unmistakably – along the Strip. Here are a few highlights from across Vegas' architectural arc.

SYLVAIN SONNET/GETTY IMAGES ©

Best Replica Architecture

Paris Las Vegas With scale-versions of the Eiffel Tower and the Arc de Triomphe, this brightly shining behemoth brings Light City to Sin City. (p40)

New York–New York NYNY is the next best thing to actually visiting the Big Apple, thanks to its Statue of Liberty and other replicas. (p30)

Luxor Prepare for your audience with the Sphinx in this giant glass pyramid that shoots out the world's strongest light beam. (p57)

Venetian Sip cappuccino on St Mark's Sq amid grand canals and a towering campanile. (p44)

Caesars Palace As outlandish as its namesake,

this mini-colosseum brims with Roman statuary, including a 25ft statue of Fortuna. (Pictured; p54)

Best Downtown Architecture

El Cortez This heritage-listed 1941 classic is festooned with original neon. (p111)

Mob Museum Study up on Capone, Bugsy and their fellow mobsters in this neoclassical former courthouse. (p102)

Fremont Street Experience Under the modern frame, a historic theater – El Portal, dating from 1928 – still stands. (p111)

Neon Museum Enter the 'neon boneyard' via the restored lobby of the La Concha Hotel, a shell-shaped mid-century beauty. (p109)

Best Edgy Architecture

CityCenter This sleek, blue-glassed complex has to be appreciated for its sheer enormity alone. (p36)

Wynn & Encore Casinos Effortlessly elegant and graceful, these marvels of modern architecture showcase Vegas' design at its best. (p48)

Container Park Urban fashion, art and drinking complex built from shipping containers and festooned with the 'Praying Mantis' sculpture. (p105)

Cosmopolitan Arguably the coolest joint in town, chic Cosmo's fantastic lobby doles out a dose of fun and eye-candy galore. (p37)

Best
Shopping

Surprisingly, Vegas has evolved into a sophisticated shopping destination. International purveyors of haute couture on the Strip cater to cashed-up clientele, whether it's catwalk fashions fresh off the runways, diamond jewels once worn by royalty or sports cars. But Sin City is still the kind of place where porn-star-worthy bling, Elvis wigs and other tacky souvenirs fly off the shelves.

What to Buy

If all you want is a T-shirt, bumper sticker or shot glass to show you've been to 'Fabulous Las Vegas,' cheap souvenirs are everywhere. If you're looking for something more unusual, the city's specialty shops are full of cool kitsch and collectibles, from vintage casino memorabilia to showgirls' feather boas.

Glamour Shopping

The Strip's high-octane shopping action is dominated by megamalls such as the Fashion Show and the Grand Canal Shoppes at the Venetian and Palazzo. Upscale boutiques also await inside CityCenter's airy Crystals mall (pictured) and luxe casino resorts like Wynn & Encore, Palazzo and Bellagio. Meanwhile, the hip Cosmopolitan casino resort collects the Strip's most eclectic indie and designer shops.

Off-Strip Finds

Downtown you'll find tacky souvenirs, but also cool vintage-clothing stores, antiques shops and art galleries, especially on Fremont St east of Las Vegas Blvd and in the 18b Arts District. West of the Strip, stock up on naughty adult toys, trashy lingerie and go-go boots. East of the Strip near University of Nevada Las Vegas, Maryland Pkwy is chock-a-block with cheap shops.

JAMES MATTIL/SHUTTERSTOCK ©

Best Fashion

Fashion Show 'The Cloud,' a futuristic-looking steel canopy, tops off this giant and flashy mall that hosts live catwalk shows. (p71)

Grand Canal Shoppes at the Palazzo Anchored by the three-story department store Barneys New York, the Palazzo's shops are dazzling. (p46)

Grand Canal Shoppes at the Venetian This airy Italianate mall adorned with frescoes has over 80 luxury boutiques. (p46)

Shops at Cosmopolitan Hipster-loving boutiques gather inside the Cosmopolitan resort. (p72)

Shopping at Bellagio (p22)

Best Shopping Malls

Shops at Crystals The most striking shopping center on the Strip for those with cash to burn. (p71)

Miracle Mile Shops A 1.2-mile-long mall with over 170 retailers and some of the US' best department stores. (p72)

Shops at Forum Trendy labels in a swish Roman marketplace anchored by a giant aquarium and a hilarious animatronic show. (p72)

Best Only-in-Vegas Shops

Gamblers General Store Nevada's largest inventory of vintage and new slot machines! (p115)

Rainbow Feather Dyeing Co A fabulous selection of feathers and fans for showgirls, in every possible hue. (p115)

Bonanza Gift Shop It's a blast wading through this enormous, tacky selection of souvenirs. (p73)

Williams Costume Company Friendly staff have supplied the Strip's aspiring starlets with DIY costuming goods since 1957. (p115)

Houdini's Magic Shop Get your magician memorabilia and DIY magic kits here. (p73)

Worth a Trip

Oozing sophistication, **Downtown Summerlin** (702-832-1000; www.downtownsummerlin.com; 1980 Festival Plaza Dr; 10am-9pm Mon-Sat, 11am-7pm Sun; 206, SX) is one of Las Vegas' most attractive outdoor shopping, dining and recreational complexes, filled with fancy boutiques and bigger department stores like Macy's and Dillard's. On Saturdays, it hosts a fantastic farmers market.

Best
Nightlife

SYLVAIN SONNET/GETTY IMAGES ©

It's no secret that Las Vegas is party central – the Strip is ground zero for some of the country's hottest clubs and most happening bars, where you never know who you'll be rubbing shoulders with. But what you might not know is that Downtown's Fremont East Entertainment District is the go-to place for Vegas' coolest nonmainstream haunts.

Hitting the Clubs

No expense has been spared to bring nightclubs in the Strip's megaresorts on a par with Los Angeles and New York City. Wildly extravagant dancefloors are like a Hollywood set designer's dream. Many clubs tend to play it safe, spinning mainstream grooves and mash-ups, but top-tier nightspots also jet in famous DJs from North America, Europe and beyond. In summer, daytime pool clubs are all the rage. Expect killer DJs, bikini-clad cocktail servers and a less-is-more dress code.

Getting Past the Velvet Rope

Typical cover charges at nightclubs are $50 on weekends and $20 on weeknights, with women usually paying less. VIP and front-of-the-line passes are sold on websites such as www.vegas.com. Also check the club's website for guest list spots or make VIP bottle-service reservations.

Raising the Bar

Many bars stay open until the wee hours, and some never close. There's also an extremely liberal policy when it comes to drinking in public, especially on the Strip and at Downtown's Fremont Street Experience.

Cocktail Bars

Skyfall Lounge Sit and sip cocktails and gaze upon spectacular sunsets over the Spring Mountains. (p27)

Parasol Up & Parasol Down It doesn't get much more stylish than this plush, two-level cocktail bar, at Wynn. (p50)

Chandelier Lounge Shimmering strands of glass beads connect three floors of cocktail wizardry at this ab-fab lounge. (p68)

Downtown Cocktail Room Classic cocktails and modern twists make this low-lit speakeasy undeniably romantic. (p114)

Encore Beach Club (p67)

Best Nightclubs

Drai's Beachclub & Nightclub Legendary after-hours parties are known for an outrageous bottle list and celebrity drop-ins. (p67)

Hakkasan Unstoppable resident DJs Tiësto and Steve Aoki rule the roost of VIP booths and floor-to-ceiling LEDs. (p64)

XS Heavyweight deck-smiths rule the dance-floor while highrollers pose at private poolside cabanas. (p66)

Surrender An outrageously gorgeous pool bar with saffron silk, yellow leather and an appropriately sexy crowd. (p66)

Jewel The successor to Aria's Haze offers a more intimate alternative to the megaclubs. (p65)

Best Rooftop Bars

Commonwealth Too cool for school? No way! Plush booths, softly chandeliers and a killer rooftop patio. (p105)

107 SkyLounge Las Vegas' highest cocktail bar is the perfect place to pop the question. (p66)

Beer Park Beneath the Eiffel Tower, overlooking the Fountains of Bellagio and countless beers on tap. (p41)

Skyfall Lounge Un-paralleled views of the southern Strip from atop Mandalay Bay's Delano hotel. (p27)

Best Pool Bars

Mandalay Bay Beach Eleven acres of beach, 2700 tons of Californian sand and up to 6ft waves. Gnarly! (p27)

Wet Republic Think of MGM Grand's 'ultra pool' as a nightclub brought into the light of day. (p66)

Encore Beach Club It doesn't get more exotic or exclusive than this decadent beach club. (p67)

Marquee From late spring through early fall, Cosmo's megapopular daytime pool club rocks the rooftop above the Strip. (p65)

Best
Casinos

You're on your third martini. You just won the last three hands. Adrenaline pumping, you double down – and lose the down payment on your next car. Gambling is no question part of the Vegas experience. Have fun, but understand the games you're playing and stop when you're ahead.

The House Always Wins

For every game except poker, the house has a statistical winning edge over the gambler and for nearly every payout, the house 'holds' a small portion of the winnings. Amounts vary with the game and with individual bets, but over the long haul, you're guaranteed to lose everything that you gamble.

Know When to Hold 'Em

Traditional casino games include poker, blackjack, baccarat, craps, roulette and slot machines. You must be at least 21 years old to play or even hang around in a casino. Every game has its own customs, traditions and strategies. Almost all casinos hand out written guides to show how to play the game and may offer free one-hour lessons in table games. Taught by pros, these include Texas Hold'em, blackjack and dice rollin' craps.

Slot Action

Slots are wildly popular and the simplest games of all to play – you just put money in and pull the handle (or push a button). The probabilities are programmed into the machine, and the chances of winning (or, more likely, losing) are the same on every pull. Careful: in Sin City, these money-gobbling machines are nicknamed 'one-armed bandits' for a reason.

RZESZUTKO/SHUTTERSTOCK ©

☑ Top Tips

▶ If you're a novice, get your feet wet with low-stakes craps.

▶ Drinks are free when you're playing, but don't forget to tip the server at least $1 per drink.

▶ The cheapest table games – and highest concentration of local gamblers – are Downtown.

Best for Highrollers

Wynn & Encore Casinos
The sassy Wynn and Encore sisters boast in excess of 1900 gaming machines and 160 tables. (p48)

Palazzo The younger sibling and extension of the Venetian is a true high-roller's casino. Together

Aria (p37)

they form Vegas' largest gaming floor. (p44)

Cosmopolitan Cosmo's gaming area is the only one in Vegas with floor-to-ceiling windows overlooking the Strip. (p37)

Aria Aria's sleek casino floor with almost 2000 slot machines might overwhelm. (p37)

Bellagio This luxurious casino with its famous fountain show featured in the 2001 remake of *Ocean's Eleven*. (p22)

Mandalay Bay Poolside slots and a luxe, resortlike atmosphere set Mandalay Bay apart. (p26)

Best Sightseeing

Golden Nugget Home of the 'Hand of Faith,' the heftiest hunk of gold ever dug up. (p100)

Hard Rock Showcasing what may be the most-impressive collection of rock-star memorabilia under one roof. (p76)

Caesars Palace The Roman Empire–inspired resort served as the setting for *The Hangover*. (p54)

Circus Circus An enormous clown-shaped marquee and tent-shaped casino under a gaudily striped big top. (p56)

Luxor This might be your only chance to gamble inside a faux Egyptian pyramid. (p57)

Best for Old-School Gambling

El Cortez A smoky, retro classic with a grassroots crowd. (p111)

Main Street Station Gamble among the antiques and beneath art nouveau chandeliers. (p111)

Golden Gate A gambling hall has stood on this spot since 1906. (p110)

Best of Locals' Favorites

Palms Fans of MTV's *Real World: Las Vegas* will recognize this hyper-modern den that claims 'looser' slots than most. (p94)

Gold Coast Old-fashioned gambling lair beloved for its low-roller roulette and traditional Chinese dim sum and dumplings. (p94)

Best
Live
Entertainment

That sensory overload of blindingly bright neon lights means you've finally landed on Las Vegas Blvd. The infamous Strip has the lion's share of gigantic casino hotels, all flashily competing to lure you (and your wallet) inside, with larger-than-life production shows, celebrity-filled night-clubs and burlesque cabarets. Head off-Strip to find jukebox dive bars, arty cocktail lounges, strip clubs and more.

ALINA SOLOVYOVA-VINCENT/GETTY IMAGES ©

What's On

The whirling Cirque du Soleil empire keeps expanding with such recent additions as *Beatles LOVE* and *Michael Jackson ONE* as well as the fantastical variety show *Zarkana*. Old-school shows at smaller casinos feature hokey song, dance and magic numbers that often don't follow a story line. Sin City's new breed of bawdy, hilarious variety shows are staged cabaret-style in unusual venues, mostly on the Strip.

Getting Tickets

Most Vegas ticket outlets apply a commission for each ticket sold. All but the biggest-ticket shows are up for grabs in-person only at **Tix 4 Tonight** (www.tix4tonight.com), a chain of same-day, discount ticket outlets. Get in line before 10am for the best selection. The website has a list of locations. Alternatively, try **Vegas.com**, which sells tickets to high-profile and low-budget shows, special events and touring exhibitions, plus nightclub VIP and front-of-the-line passes. Of course, there's always the good-old standby **Ticketmaster** (www.ticketsmaster.com), a broker for megaconcerts and sporting events.

Best Spectacles & Shows

Le Rêve the Dream
Cirque du Soleil's surreal Dream plays out underwater in a custom-built swimming pool. (p49)

O A spectacular feat of engineering, this original aquatic masterpiece explores the history of theater. (p24)

Beatles LOVE Beatlemania is back! All your favorite tunes fused with dance and aerial acrobatics. (p68)

Michael Jackson ONE
Showstopping dancers and lithe acrobats bring MJ's greatest hits to life. (p28)

Blue Man Group Art, music, technology and comedy combine in one of Vegas' most popular, family-friendly shows. (p68)

Mirage Volcano (p57)

Best Free Entertainment

Circus Circus This cheesy casino has free circus acts and loads of family fun. (p56)

Fountains of Bellagio A visit to Vegas is incomplete without snapping these free dancing fountains. (p23)

Mirage Volcano As gaudy as it gets, this may be the closest you'll come to a volcanic eruption. (p57)

Fremont Street Experience A five-block pedestrian mall, illuminated at night and chock-full of entertainment. (p111)

Best Comedy & Magic

Penn & Teller This intellectual odd couple have struck the balance between magic and comedy. (p97)

Criss Angel Mindfreak Live Billed as the greatest magic spectacle of all time. (p70)

Carrot Top Find out why this wild, orange-haired comedian has audiences begging for more. (p70)

Best Music Venues

House of Blues This cool, Southern-style venues features live soul, pop, rock, country, jazz and, of course, blues. (p28)

Brooklyn Bowl Hip NYC import does triple duty as bowling alley, restaurant and concert venue for indie bands. (p35)

Le Cabaret Free live jazz and sultry lounge music in an intimate venue at Paris Las Vegas. (p42)

Best Major Venues

Colosseum There's hardly a bad seat in the house at Caesars Palace's 4100-seat theater-in-the-round. (p70)

Smith Center for the Performing Arts An architecturally beautiful multivenue complex in Downtown's Symphony Park. (p114)

Park Theater This brand-new, sexy, avant-garde theater pulls in A-list artists. (p70)

T-Mobile Arena In the heart of the Strip, this state-of-the-art arena, new in 2016, seats up to 20,000. (p70)

Best
Fine Dining

ETHAN MILLER/GETTY IMAGES ©

The Strip has been studded with celebrity chefs for years. All-you-can-eat buffets and $10 steaks still exist, but today's high-rolling visitors demand ever more sophisticated dining experiences, with meals designed – although not personally prepared – by famous taste-makers.

Celebs in the Kitchen

After Wolfgang Puck brought Spago to Caesars Palace in 1992, celebrity American chefs opened branches at every megaresort. Geniuses of the kitchen who have leapt onto the Strip include Bobby Flay, Mario Batali, Emeril Lagasse and Nobu Matsuhisa. Keep in mind that most have nothing to do with the day-to-day operations of their name-sake Vegas kitchens.

Scoring a Table

Most restaurants take reservations for dinner and sometimes lunch, so call ahead if you can or book online through the restaurant or the free Open-Table (www.opentable.com) website and mobile app. If all else fails, ask your hotel concierge for help and be prepared to tip $10 for a primo table reservation.

Local Eats

Where do you go when you tire of inflated casino prices? Venture to Downtown or to the east and west of the Strip where locals drink and dine for far less than what dazed tourists are shelling out on the Strip. Not only will you get better gastronomic bang for your buck, you'll be able to take a little bite of everything from authentic Thai street snacks and Neapolitan pizzas to Asian-Mexican fusion tacos and crazy food-truck creations.

Best Celebrity Chefs

Restaurant Guy Savoy You want exclusive? This is the only US restaurant by three-star Michelin chef Guy Savoy. (p60)

Joël Robuchon 'Chef of the century' Robuchon's eponymous restaurant lives up to the hype. (p60)

Border Grill Weekend brunches are best at this TV-celeb modern Mexican joint. (p61)

Guy Fieri's Vegas Kitchen & Bar *Diners, Drive-ins and Dives'* everyday hero's foray into the Vegas food scene. (Pictured; p58)

Best Table with a View

Top of the World You'll pay for the incredible

views from Vegas' highest revolving restaurant. (p62)

Todd English's Olives You can't get closer to the Fountains of Bellagio than at this smart eatery. (p64)

Twist by Pierre Gagnaire You'll gasp at the romantic views from this Michelin-hatted French restaurant. (p38)

Eiffel Tower Restaurant Perched high on the Eiffel Tower, above the Fountains of Bellagio. Say no more. (p41)

Rivea Delano's rooftop sensation has spectacular views from the southern Strip. (p62)

Best Japanese Cuisine

Raku Authenticity without celebrity reigns at this off-Strip sushi joint and *robata* grill. (p91)

Morimoto It's hard to resist TV's Iron Chef Masaharu Morimoto's inventive fusion of Japanese and American cuisine. (p60)

Nobu Iron Chef 'Nobu' Matsuhisa's sequel to his trendsetting NYC establishment. (p63)

Steakhouses

Bazaar Meat Next-gen steakhouse with global influences. (p61)

Stripsteak A stylishly minimalist steakhouse with all-natural beef and unusual gourmet sides. (p63)

SW Steakhouse Classic cuts by the side of a pint-sized lake. (p50)

Worth a Trip

A favorite with the locals in Summerlin, **Farm Basket** (☎702-878-6343; www.farmbasketlv.com; 6148 W Charleston Blvd; fried chicken $4-15; ⏱10am-9pm; P) has been in business since 1973 and is the last branch of what used to be a popular fried-chicken franchise. Secrets include chunks of turkey meat in the gravy, and orange marmalade on the buns. Yum!

Best
Local Culture

It's easy to forget that there's a city beyond the Strip – and a fascinating one at that. There's the hipster scene Downtown, where you can rub shoulders with locals at indie music venues. Nearby, vintage neon signs hark back to Vegas' early days, while west of the Strip, the impressive Springs Preserve connects you with local natural history.

LUCKYRACCOON/SHUTTERSTOCK ©

A Growing Arts Scene

Arts and culture in Las Vegas would, until recently, have been just another oxymoron. That's no longer the case, however, with a thriving Downtown arts scene, a couple of Smithsonian-affiliated museums and UNLV's Performing Arts Center all being rewarding destinations for culture vultures.

Passion for the Game

Until the Oakland Raiders football team relocates to Las Vegas (perhaps in 2018/19), the city does not have any professional sports franchises. But it does have its share of die-hard sports fans. You can wager on just about anything at race and sports books inside casinos, and nearly every watering hole runs Monday Night Football specials. World-class championship boxing draws fans from all over the globe, and weekend 'fight nights' are huge on the Strip.

Head for the Hills

Locals love the outdoors and it's easy to join them. Options suitable for easy day trips include Red Rock Canyon National Conservation Area, which has hiking and rock climbing. There's good mountain biking outside Boulder City, while Lake Mead beckons with boating, fishing and other water sports.

Best Drinking & Partying

Beauty Bar Chill with the cool kids inside this resurrected 1950s beauty-salon-cum-speakeasy in Downtown. (p105)

Double Down Saloon Mix with the lunatic fringe at this dark, psychedelic gin joint that never closes. (p86)

Commonwealth Raise your pinkie with old-fashioned cocktails on the rooftop patio or in the plush Prohibition-style interior. (p105)

Firefly Mingle with fashionable local folk over tapas and late-night drinks on the patio. (p85)

First Friday Community-arts-festival-cum-street-parties in Downtown's Arts District on...yes indeed...the first Friday of the month. (p112)

Best History

National Atomic Testing Museum Delve into Sin City's dark atomic past, when people came out for the mushroom clouds. (p80)

Pinball Hall of Fame Retro fun in a wonderland of vintage pinball machines and video games. (p84)

Welcome to Las Vegas Sign Arrive after dark for maximum 'wows' when cruising past this iconic 1950s neon sign. (p56)

Springs Preserve This educational complex is a rewarding trip through historical, cultural and biological time. (p90)

Nevada State Museum Mammoths to mobsters, Hoover Dam to atomic bombs, this museum's got Sin City's milestones covered. (p91)

Best for Watching Sports

Triple 7 Lively Monday Night Football on the screens and great microbrews on tap. (p114)

Caesars Palace One of many popular sports books in town, this area of the casino offers special menus and customized 'man caves' for major sporting events. (p54)

Mandalay Bay Events Center High-profile boxing matches, plus ultimate fighting. (p28)

Worth a Trip

Brand-name bargain hunters head to Vegas' jam-packed outlet malls. The best of the bunch is **Las Vegas Premium Outlets North** (702-474-7500; www.premiumoutlets.com/vegasnorth; 875 S Grand Central Pkwy; 9am-9pm Mon-Sat, to 8pm Sun; SDX), a retail haven with designer names including Armani, DKNY, Dolce & Gabbana and Michael Kors, along with casual brands such as True Religion and Juicy Couture.

Best
Off-Strip Dining

Those flashy restaurants on the Strip – named by celebrity chefs and offering A-listers sweeping views – get all the attention in Vegas. But the city's off-Strip gourmet scene has been quietly developing for years, attracting locals and traveling foodies for more authentic (and often better-value) dining experiences; just ask Anthony Bourdain, who chose Las Vegas for an episode of his TV show *Parts Unknown*.

PAVEL L PHOTO AND VIDEO/SHUTTERSTOCK ©

Eating Like a Local

Vegas' version of China-town, populated with a nice array of Korean, Japanese and Chinese eateries, is located a short drive west of the Strip. Downtown, opt for retro steakhouses, where you can soak up some Old Vegas charm. Hugely popular breakfast joints and tapas bars round out the list.

Best Asian

Raku Japanese *robata*-style charcoal grill featuring sake samplers. (p91)

Lotus of Siam Northern Thai cuisine and a fantastic wine list – in a strip mall. (p85)

Chinatown Plaza Hong Kong barbecue, Vietnam-ese pho shops and sushi bars in Vegas' Chinatown. (p96)

Ping Pang Pong Traditional Chinese food and dim sum. (p96)

Best Gastropubs

Carson Kitchen Industrial-flavored hipster joint with modern American share plates. (p105)

Culinary Dropout Legendary lair with pool-view patio and live bands rocking on weekends. (p77)

Best Steakhouses

Andiamo Steakhouse Detroit transplant with the look and feel of a classic, old-school steakhouse. (p113)

Golden Steer Elvis and the Rat Pack dined at this retro steakhouse. (p62)

Best Latin

Firefly The stylish locals' favorite for tapas and drinks on the patio. (p85)

La Comida The gamut of kickass Mexican favorites with lashings of tequila in a cozy setting. (p112)

Best for Breakfast

eat. Urban Downtown eatery dishes up big-flavored breakfasts made with sustainable, local and organic ingredients. (p112)

Hash House a Go Go Pancakes the size of a tractor wheel at this breakfast hot spot imported from SoCal. (p61)

Best
For Newlyweds

Of course, you don't have to elope to find romance in Sin City. Steal a kiss over cocktails at one of the city's sky-high bars, clasp hands as you watch the Bellagio's dancing fountains show, or just hide out with your paramour in a luxury suite all weekend.

PAUL BRADBURY/GETTY IMAGES ©

Las Vegas for Lovers

Whether or not you're planning to tie the knot, it's no secret that Sin City is practically made for lovers – at least those who don't take themselves too seriously. Room service menus feature champagne, gourmet chocolate and x-rated goodies should you need help to get in the mood. High-end restaurants and bars feature cozy seating and dining areas ideal for a romantic rendezvous, while chapels – both freestanding and located within the resorts – specialize in walk-up weddings, just in case the mood strikes.

Mention to the hotel receptionist that you're on a romantic getaway and you'll be offered add-ons from whirlpool tubs to rose petals strewn across the bed at turndown time. The cheesy 'Just Married' accessories for sale around town aren't just a kitschy souvenir: you're bound to enjoy a few free drinks if you're wearing them when you walk through the Strip's bars and casinos.

Best for Newlyweds

Gondola Ride Float along the Venetian's canals, or under a moonlit lake. (p45)

Graceland Wedding Chapel Seal the deal where Jon Bon Jovi did. Elvis impersonator optional. (p112)

Qua Baths & Spa A gorgeous spa fit for brides-to-be or honeymooners. (p55)

Mandarin Bar & Tea Lounge Toast the future with tea or bubbles overlooking the Strip. (p68)

Eiffel Tower Experience Imagine you're honeymooning in the City of Lights. (p41)

Vegas Weddings The only drive-thru wedding window in the city, plus a pretty mini-cathedral. (p112)

Spa by Mandara Couples can opt for the romantic 'Paris for Lovers' treatment package, delivered with a whirlpool tub made for two. (p42)

La Cave At this intimate lair with archways and candlelight, you can pretend you're having tapas and wine in Barcelona. (p58)

Parasol Up & Parasol Down Memorable venues for a romantic rendezvous over artisan cocktails. (p50)

Best
For Kids

Las Vegas may be a bit too *sinful* to be truly family-friendly. But if you look past the smoke and glitter – which admittedly is hard to do in this town – you'll notice a range of attractions and activities suitable for all ages.

MARK GIBSON/GETTY IMAGES ©

Most casinos have virtual-reality and video-game arcades, some have roller coasters and thrill rides and shows suitable for the entire family abound as well. To get off the Strip and into a slightly more natural environment, head to the Park or LINQ Promenade, where there's plenty of kid-friendly stuff to do. For eats, look for casino and shopping mall food courts.

Best Thrills & Rides

Big Apple Roller Coaster Hold onto your hat aboard this Coney Island–style coaster at New York–New York. (Pictured; p31)

Adventuredome Get your kicks with thrill rides, rock climbing and bungee jumping below the pink-glass panes of this

indoor amusement park at Circus Circus. (p56)

Stratosphere Feed your teen with adrenaline on the world's highest thrill rides, 110 stories above the Strip. (p55)

Slotzilla Courageous kids will beg to ride this zipline suspended 12 stories above the Fremont Street Experience. (p111)

Best Shows

Mirage Volcano Visible from the Strip, the faux volcano's molten explosions are entertaining for all ages. (p57)

Fremont Street Experience A five-block pedestrian mall topped by an arched steel canopy and filled with computer-controlled lights. (p111)

Best Animal Attractions

Shark Reef Aquarium For an audience with

fishy friends, head to this walk-through aquarium teeming with over 2000 exotic submarine beasties. (p27)

Flamingo Wildlife Habitat Prancing flamingos and waddling penguins are among the denizens of this exotic mini-zoo. (p57)

Best Kid-Friendly Exhibits

Discovery Children's Museum Experiment, paint, study scientific concepts or play dress-up in this colorful interactive play-and-learn space. (p110)

Springs Preserve Detour from the Strip for a breath of fresh air and a fix of eco-conscious design at this educational museum complex. (p90)

Survival Guide

Before You Go   **148**

When to Go 148
Book Your Stay 148

Arriving in Las Vegas   **150**

McCarran International Airport 150
Driving into Las Vegas 150

Getting Around   **150**

Bus 150
Car & Motorcycle 151
Monorail 151
Shuttle 151
Taxi & Limousine 152
Tram 152

Essential Information   **152**

Business Hours 152
Discounts 152
Electricity 152
Emergency 153
Gay & Lesbian Travelers 153
Money 153
Public Holidays 153
Safe Travel 153
Tourist Information 154
Travelers with Disabilities 154
Visas 154

Survival Guide

Before You Go

When to Go

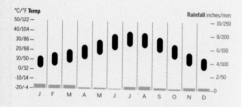

°C/°F Temp
Rainfall inches/mm

➡ **Spring (Mar–May)**
Perfect weather and steady crowds; the conference set will be reserving blocks of hotel rooms.

➡ **Summer (Jun–Aug)**
Dog days of summer. Too hot to enjoy outdoor activities, except at night.

➡ **Fall (Sep & Oct)**
Balmy temperatures make Vegas a pleasant getaway. Hotel room competition heats up with plenty of conferences in town.

➡ **Winter (Nov–Feb)**
The chilliest time of year; the famous pool bars shut down during these months.

Book Your Stay

Useful Websites

Lonely Planet (www.lonelyplanet.com/hotels) Book hotels and other accommodations.

Vegas.com (www.vegas.com) Local online travel agent exclusively servicing Las Vegas.

Travelzoo (www.travelzoo com) For discount hotel deals.

Priceline (www.priceline.com) Lets you bid or 'express' buy your hotel room for less.

Travelworm (www.travelworm.com) Comprehensive hotel listings and promos.

Best Budget

Downtown Grand (www.downtowngrand.com) Good-value digs in the heart of Downtown.

Golden Nugget (www.goldennugget.com) This local legend wins top points for Downtown's best rooms and amenities.

El Cortez (www.elcortezhotelcasino.com) For something a little different, where old meets new Downtown.

Hard Rock (www.hardrockhotel.com) Off-Strip party palace for music lovers with sexy, oversized rooms.

Thunderbird Hotel (www.thunderbirdhotellasvegas.com) Funky, fresh rooms with reclaimed-wood furniture and a fun, youthful vibe.

Best Midrange

LINQ Hotel (www.caesars.com/linq) You can't go past LINQ for value and its center-Strip location.

SLS (www.slslasvegas.com) A north Strip location means incredible rates for this boutique brand.

Platinum Hotel & Spa (www.theplatinumhotel.com) This nongaming, nonsmoking hotel near the Strip has sanctuary-like suites.

Aria Las Vegas Resort (www.arialasvegas.com) Sleek resort hotel where every room has a corner view.

W Las Vegas (www.wlasvegas.com) If you like design and a cooler crowd, hang at this 2017 newcomer.

Best Top End

Encore (www.wynnlasvegas.com) Excellence at every turn.

Signature at MGM Grand (www.signaturemgmgrand.com) Indulgent suites atop the massive megalopolis of MGM Grand.

Four Seasons Hotel (www.fourseasons.com/lasvegas) Fresh from renovation, Mandalay Bay's luxury offering doesn't fail to impress.

Mandarin Oriental (www.mandarinoriental.com) Luscious oriental flavors meet the latest technology.

Cosmopolitan (www.cosmopolitanlasvegas.com) Hippest Strip rooms with sunken tubs, balconies and design quirks.

Money-Saving Tips

➡ If you're trying to lock in a good rate at a popular resort, call the hotel directly and ask about special promotions or better rates on unremodeled rooms.

➡ Don't make room reservations on the weekend; rates often drop across the board on Monday mornings.

➡ For live entertainment, save cash by scoring last-minute tickets at **Tix4Tonight** (www.tix4tonight.com).

➡ Take advantage of such free attractions as the Fountains at Bellagio, the Burlesque Hall of Fame, the Mirage Volcano, the Fremont Street Experience and the outdoor Neon Museum.

➡ Get free drinks while playing the slots (but do tip).

Be Forewarned

Smoking If cigarette smoke bothers you, steer clear of older casinos and gamble at the airier Wynn/Encore, Venetian/Palazzo or Bellagio.

Sex workers Prostitution is illegal in Clark County, but escorts, call girls and working girls are part of Sin City's high-rolling culture.

Resort fees Think you scored a deal on your hotel room? Most hotels add mandatory daily 'resort fees' of $10 to $30, which may cover internet access and fitness-center entry, or nothing much at all. Some also charge $10 for phone reservations.

Arriving in Las Vegas

McCarran International Airport

→ The easiest and cheapest way to get to your hotel is by airport shuttle (one-way to Strip/downtown hotels from $7/9) or a shared ride-share service like Uber or Lyft (from $10). As you exit baggage claim, look for shuttle bus kiosks lining the curb; prices and destinations are clearly marked.

→ Taxis hover at $15 to $25 for the Strip and upwards of $20 for Downtown, plus tip.

→ If you're renting a car from the airport, catch a shuttle bus outside baggage claim to the McCarran Rent-a-Car Center.

Driving into Las Vegas

→ The main roads into and out of Las Vegas are the I-15 Fwy and US Hwy 95. US Hwy 93 connects Downtown with Hoover Dam. I-215 goes by McCarran International Airport.

→ When traffic is snarled on I-15 and Las Vegas Blvd, stick to surface routes, such as Paradise Rd, east of the Strip; or Frank Sinatra Dr and Industrial Rd, west of the Strip.

→ The fastest way to get across the Strip and I-15 is via the Desert Inn Rd super-arterial.

Getting Around

Bus

→ **RTC** (Regional Transportation Commission of Southern Nevada; ☎702-228-7433, 800-228-3911; www.rtcsnv.com/transit; single ride $2, 2/24/72hr bus pass $6/8/20, child under 5yr free) buses operate from 5am to 2am daily, with popular Strip and Downtown routes running 24/7 every 15 to 20 minutes. RTC's double-decker Deuce buses to/

Walking the Strip

The Strip runs for miles: don't assume you can easily walk from point A to B. Consult a map first and note that pedestrian crossings are punctuated with sky bridges and escalators. Take advantage of free trams between casinos whenever possible.

from Downtown stop every block or two along the Strip; quicker SDX (Strip & Downtown Express) buses stop outside some Strip casino hotels, as well as at the Fashion Show, the city's convention center and a few off-Strip shopping malls.

➡ Many off-Strip casino hotels offer limited shuttle buses to/from the Strip, usually reserved for hotel guests.

Car & Motorcycle

➡ Driving on the Strip can be stressful. As of April 2017, self-parking at Strip casinos is no longer free.

➡ International short-term visitors only need their home license to rent or drive a car or motorcycle. If your license isn't written in English, you may be required to show an international driving permit (IDP).

What to Bring

Classy clothes Women can get away with jeans, but a dress code is loosely enforced at the best nightclubs and restaurants.

Comfortable shoes If you want to explore the Strip, you'll need something supportive.

Camera Be prepared to snap.

Aspirin or ibuprofen For morning-after aches and pains.

Monorail

➡ The **Las Vegas Monorail** (📞702-699-8299; www.lvmonorail.com; single ride $5, 24/72hr pass $12/28; ⏰7am-midnight Mon, to 2am Tue-Thu, to 3am Fri-Sun) links some Strip casino-resorts, zipping between MGM Grand, Bally's/Paris, Flamingo/Caesars, Harrah's/LINQ, Las Vegas Convention Center, Westgate and SLS/W.

➡ Although service is frequent (every four to 12 minutes), stations are only on the east side of the Strip, set back from Las Vegas Blvd at the rear of the casinos.

➡ Trains are air-conditioned and stroller- and wheelchair-friendly.

Shuttle

➡ Many off-Strip casino hotels offer limited free shuttle buses to and from the Strip, although some are reserved for hotel guests.

➡ Free public shuttles connect the Rio with Harrah's and Bally's/Paris Las Vegas usually every

Renting a Car

Booking online through a car-rental agency or a discount travel website normally nets you the best rates. Economy car-rental rates start at $25/145 per day/week, though you might find a much cheaper deal by surfing the web ahead of time. Expect to pay extra for insurance (usually optional), taxes of over 10% and government surcharges of 10%. A facility charge (almost $4 per day) and 10% airport fee often apply as well. Most companies require a major credit card, and some require that the driver be at least 25 years old.

30 minutes from 10am until 1am daily.

Taxi & Limousine

➡ It's illegal to hail a cab on the street. Instead, taxi stands are found at almost every casino hotel and shopping mall.

➡ Vegas is surprisingly compact, so taxis can be reasonable on a per-trip basis. A lift from one end of the Strip to the other, or from mid-Strip to Downtown, costs at least $20, depending on traffic.

➡ Tip the driver 10% to 15%, rounded up to the nearest dollar.

➡ For special occasions or stepping out in style, some parties will hire a limousine. Popular companies include Presidential Limo.

➡ A good resource is www.vegas.com/transportation/las-vegas-taxis.

Tram

Free public air-conditioned trams shuttle all day long between some Strip casino hotels. One connects the Bellagio, CityCenter and the Monte Carlo. Another links Treasure Island and the Mirage. A third zips between Excalibur, Luxor and Mandalay Bay.

Essential Information

....

Business Hours

Bars 5pm–3am as a general rule.

Casinos 24 hours year-round.

Restaurants hours vary wildly, but generally 11am–2pm for lunch and 5pm–10pm for dinner.

Shops 10am–9pm (to 6pm Sunday), closed Christmas Day; to 11pm in casinos.

Discounts

➡ Check **Smarter Vegas** (www.smartervegas.com) for promotional discount codes for sights, tours, shows and hotels.

➡ A multiday **Las Vegas Power Pass** (www.lasvegaspowerpass.com) may be worthwhile if you plan to visit a lot of big-ticket attractions and museums; it even lets you skip the lines at some of them.

Electricity

Type A
120V/60Hz

Type B
120V/60Hz

Emergency

Police, fire, ambulance (☎911)

Gay & Lesbian Travelers

Let's be clear: it's perfectly OK to be 'out' in Vegas. It's a place where you can be who you are and even be who you wanna be, but as with most places, don't be surprised if wildly flamboyant behavior is met with rudeness or disdain. Americans are generally friendly, respectful people. Respect the rules and behaviors of those around you, and you'll inevitably be treated in the same way.

Money

➡ All casinos, banks, shopping malls, and most convenience stores, have ATMs.

➡ Cold hard cash greases Sin City's wheels. You'll want to have bills of various sizes on hand, partly so you're ready to tip when necessary.

➡ Casinos charge ridiculous rates for currency exchange.

➡ Credit cards are widely accepted. All casinos will advance cash against

plastic but fees are exorbitant.

Public Holidays

Note that the only holiday that shops always close for is Christmas.

New Year's Day January 1

Martin Luther King Jr Day Third Monday in January

Presidents' Day Third Monday in February

Good Friday Friday before Easter in March/April

Memorial Day Last Monday in May

Independence Day July 4

Labor Day First Monday in September

Columbus Day Second Monday in October

Veterans Day November 11

Tips on Tipping

Keep small bills on hand. Leave a poor tip for remarkably lousy service, or in exceptionally bad (rare) cases, none at all. Reward exceptional service. Minimum tipping standards:

Hotels Porters: $1 to $2 per bag; housekeeping $1 to $2 per night; valet $2 to $5 (paid when keys returned)

Restaurants 15% to 25% of total bill

Bars/casinos $1 per drink or 15% per round

Taxis/limos 15% of fare, at your discretion

Thanksgiving Day Fourth Thursday in November

Christmas Day December 25

Safe Travel

➡ On the Strip and the Fremont Street Experience, police and private security officers are out in force, and surveillance cameras ('eyes in the sky') are omnipresent.

➡ Utilize in-room hotel safes and never leave valuables unattended, especially while gambling.

➡ Beware of pickpockets in crowds (eg on public transportation).

➡ If you wander Downtown away from Fremont St, keep your wits about you, day and

The Lowdown on Smoking

'Smoke-free' and 'Las Vegas' are rarely mentioned in the same sentence: there are ashtrays at almost every telephone, elevator, swimming pool – even in toilets and taxis. A limited ban on smoking inside public buildings, including restaurants, shops and movie theaters, went into effect in 2006, but exceptions still permit smoking inside casinos, as well as at bars and clubs that don't serve prepared food. Most casino hotels claim to offer nonsmoking rooms, but don't expect the air to be free of a whiff of cigarettes.

night. Likewise, the area between Downtown and the Stratosphere can be sketchy.

Tourist Information

➡ The **Las Vegas Convention & Visitors Authority** (LVCVA; Map p52; ☎ 702-892-7575; www. lasvegas.com; 3150 Paradise Rd; ⏰ 8am-5:30pm Mon-Fri; 💻 Las Vegas Convention Center) hotline provides up-to-date information about shows, attractions, activities and more; staff may help with finding last-minute accommodations.

➡ Check out www. vegas.com for additional tourist resources and bookings.

Travelers with Disabilities

➡ Vegas has the most ADA-accessible guestrooms in the USA. Almost all attractions are wheelchair-accessible.

➡ Wheelchair seating is widely available and assisted listening devices are offered at most showrooms.

➡ Most public transportation and several hotel pools are lift-equipped.

➡ By law, all taxi companies must have a wheelchair-accessible van.

Visas

The following information is highly subject to change. Double-check visa and passport requirements at http:// travel.state.gov or with

a US consulate in your country before coming to the USA.

➡ Visas aren't required for citizens of the 37 Visa Waiver Program (VWP) countries, who may enter the USA for up to 90 days visa-free.

➡ However, citizens of these countries must still apply for travel authorization online (see https:// esta.cbp.dhs.gov) at least 72 hours before traveling; registration is usually valid for two years. VWP travelers must also be in possession of a round-trip or onward ticket to enter the US. Passports must meet current US standards.

➡ Temporary visitors from Canada do not normally need a visa for stays of up to 181 days, but they must bring their Canadian passport.

➡ All other foreign citizens must wrangle a nonimmigrant visa in advance from a US embassy or consulate. Best done in your home country, the process costs a nonrefundable fee (minimum $160), involves a personal interview and can take several weeks, so apply early.

Behind the Scenes

Send Us Your Feedback

We love to hear from travelers – your comments help make our books better. We read every word, and we guarantee that your feedback goes straight to the authors. Visit **lonelyplanet.com/contact** to submit your updates and suggestions.

Note: We may edit, reproduce and incorporate your comments in Lonely Planet products such as guidebooks, websites and digital products, so let us know if you don't want your comments reproduced or your name acknowledged. For a copy of our privacy policy visit lonelyplanet.com/privacy.

Benedict's Thanks

A huge thank you to Alex Howard from LP for granting me this amazing opportunity and sticking by me until I got 'er done. I dedicate this update to Mr and Mrs Bruce and Cheryl Cowie, my self-adopted Canadian parents and the original high rollers of my world. Thanks to Mum for giving Nanna's prayer-chair a workout; to Kirk, Alex and friends for showing me their Vegas; to Justin and the burners in Reno, my birthday buddy Nicole in Carson city, and my favorite American, Brad, for speaking my language and keeping me sane. You all rock.

Acknowledgements

Cover photograph: The Strip, Yaacov Dagan/Alamy ©
Contents photograph: New York–New York, Mitch Diamond/Getty ©

This Book

This 5th edition of Lonely Planet's *Pocket Las Vegas* guidebook was curated by Andrea Schulte-Peevers, and researched and written by Benedict Walker. The previous edition was written by Bridget Gleeson. This guidebook was produced by the following:

Destination Editor Alexander Howard **Product Editor** Heather Champion **Senior Cartographer** Alison Lyall

Book Designer Katherine Marsh **Assisting Editors** Michelle Bennett, Anne Mulvaney **Cover Researcher** Marika Mercer **Thanks to** Shona Gray, Wayne Murphy, Kathryn Rowan, Saralinda Turner, Tony Wheeler

Index

See also separate subindexes for:

- ⊗ **Eating** p158
- ⊙ **Drinking** p158
- ✿ **Entertainment** p159
- 🔒 **Shopping** p159

18b 107, *see also* Arts District

A
accommodations 148-9
Adventuredome 56
Alan Bible Visitor Center 122
ambulance 153
architecture 131
Aria 37-8
Aria Fine Art Collection 37
Art Square 107
Arts District 107
Arts Factory 107
ATMs 153

B
Bellagio 22-5, **25**
Bellagio Conservatory & Botanical Gardens 23-4
Bellagio Gallery of Fine Art 24
Big Apple Arcade 31
Big Apple Roller Coaster 31
Binion's Gambling Hall 110
Boulder City 122
buffets 130

Sights 000
Map Pages **000**

Burlesque Hall of Fame 107, 111
bus travel 150-1
business hours 152

C
Caesars Palace 54-5
Canyon Ranch SpaClub 46
Canyon Vistas Mule Rides 118
car travel 151
casinos 136-7
cell phones 14
chefs, celebrity 140
    Andrés, José 60, 61
    Ducasse, Alain 62
    English, Todd 38, 64
    Fieri, Guy 58
    Gagnaire, Pierre 38
    Matsuhisa, Nobu 63
    Mina, Michael 63
    Morimoto, Masaharu 60
    Ramsay, Gordon 35, 42
    Robuchon, Joël 60
    Rochat, André 96
    Savoy, Guy 60-1
    Wu, Kevin 96
children, travel with 146
Circus Circus 56
Cirque du Soleil
    Kà 54
    Michael Jackson ONE 28

O 24
Zumanity 32
CityCenter 36-9, **39**
CityCenter Fine Art Collection 37
climate 148
clothing 72
Container Park 105
Cosmopolitan 37
costs 14, 149, 152
credit cards 153
culture 142-3
currency 14

D
dangers, *see* safety
Desert Adventures 122
Desert Living Center 91
Desert View Watchtower 117
disabilities, travelers with 154
Discovery Children's Museum 110
Downtown & Fremont Street 98-115, **108**
    drinking 113-4
    entertainment 114-5
    food 112-3
    itineraries 99, 104-7
    shopping 115
    sights 100-3, 109-12
    transportation 99
dress codes 72
drinking 134-5, 142,

see also individual neighborhoods, Drinking *subindex*

E
East of the Strip 74-87, **82-3**
    drinking 86-7
    entertainment 87
    food 84-6
    itineraries 75
    shopping 87
    sights 76-81, 84
    transportation 75
Eiffel Tower Experience 41
El Cortez 111
electricity 152
emergencies 153
entertainment 138-9, *see also* Entertainment *subindex*

F
fire 153
First Fridays 107, 112
Flamingo Wildlife Habitat 57
flights, scenic 118
food 130, 140-1, 144, *see also* chefs, celebrity, *individual casinos, individual neighborhoods,* Eating *subindex*
Fountains of Bellagio 23

Fremont, John C 95
Fremont Street Experience 111
Fruit Loop 87

G
gangsters 69
gay travelers 87
Gold Coast 94
Golden Gate 110
Golden Nugget 100-1
Gondola Ride 45-6
Graceland Wedding Chapel 112
Grand Canyon 116-19
Grand Canyon Airlines 118

H
Hand of Faith 101
Hard Rock Hotel & Casino 76
highlights 8-11
High Roller 35
hiking 118, 122
history 69, 95, 123, 143
holidays 153
honeymoons 145
Hoover Dam 120-3
Hoover Dam Museum 121

I
itineraries 12-13, 126-9, *see also individual neighborhoods*

K
kayaking 122

L
Lake Mead 120-3
Lake Mead Cruises 122
Lake Mead National Recreation Area 121

language 14
lesbian travelers 87
LGBT travelers 87
limousines 152
LINQ Casino 54
LINQ Promenade 34-5
Luxor 57

M
Main Street Station 111
Mandalay Bay 26-9, **29**
Mandalay Bay Beach 27
Mandarin Oriental 38
MGM Grand 54
Mike O'Callaghan-Pat Tillman Memorial Bridge 121
Mirage 57
Mirage Volcano 57
Mob Museum 102-3
Mob, the 69
mobile phones 14
money 14, 149, 152, 153
monorail 151
Mormons 95
motorcycle travel 151

N
National Atomic Testing Museum 80-1
Neon Museum (Neon Boneyard) 109
Neon Museum - Urban Gallery 109-10
Nevada National Security Site 81
Nevada State Museum 91
New York-New York 30-3, **33**
newlyweds 145
nightlife 64, 134-5

O
opening hours 152
Origen Museum 91

P
packing 151
Palazzo 44-7, **47**
Palms 94
Papillon Grand Canyon Helicopters 118
Paris Las Vegas 40-3, **43**
Park 56
Pinball Hall of Fame 84
Plaza 110
Polaroid Museum 35
police 153
prostitution 84, 114, 150
public holidays 153

Q
Qua Baths & Spa 55

R
Reliquary Spa & Salon 78
Rideshare services 68
Rim Trail 118
Rio 94

S
safety 153-4
sex workers 84, 114, 150
Shark Reef Aquarium 27-8
Shark Tank 101
shopping 132-3, *see also individual neighborhoods*, Shopping *subindex*
shuttle buses 151-2
Siegel, Benjamin 'Bugsy' 69

Sinatra, Frank 69
Slotzilla 111
SLS 57
smoking 150, 154
Southern Paiute people 95
Spa at Encore 50
Spa Bellagio 24
Spa by Mandara 42
sports 142, 143
Springs Preserve 90-1
Stratosphere 54
Stratosphere Thrill Rides 55
street art 107
Strip, the 20-73, **52-3**
   drinking 64-8
   entertainment 68, 70
   food 57-64
   itineraries 21
   shopping 71-3
   sights 22-51, 54-7
   transportation 21

T
taxis 152
telephone services 14
tickets 64, 70
time 14
tipping 14, 153
top sights 8-11
tram travel 152
transportation 15, 150-2

V
Valley of Fire 112
Vdara 38
Vegas Mob Tour 84
Vegas Watersports 122
Vegas Weddings 112
Venetian 44-7, **47**
visas 14, 154
VooDoo ZipLine 94

W

walking 150
walks 126-9, 150
watersports 122
weather 148
websites 14, 148-9
weddings 112, 145
Welcome to Las Vegas Sign 56
West of the Strip 88-97, **92-3**
   drinking 96-7
   entertainment 97
   food 94, 96
   itineraries 89
   sights 90-1, 94
   transportation 89
Wynn & Encore Casinos 48-51, 51
Wynn, Steve 24

✖ Eating

A

Alizé 96
Andiamo Steakhouse 113

B

Bacchanal 62
Bazaar Meat 61
Border Grill 61
Bouchon 46
Buffet at Bellagio 64
Buffet at Wynn 62
Burger Bar 59

C

Carnival World Buffet 96
Carson Kitchen 105
Chart House 101
China Poblano 60
Chinatown Plaza 96
Coffee Cup 122
Container Park 105
Costa di Mare 50
Cravings 60
Culinary Dropout 77

E

eat. 112
Eiffel Tower Restaurant 41
El Tovar 118
Envy 86
Evel Pie 103

F

Farm Basket 141
Fat Choy 84
Firefly 85
Flippin' Good Burgers & Fries 103

G

Gallagher's Steakhouse 32
Gold Coast 94
Golden Steer 62
Gordon Ramsay Fish & Chips 35
Gordon Ramsay Steak 42
Grand Canyon Lodge Dining Room 118
Grand Wok 58-9
Guy Fieri's Vegas Kitchen & Bar 58

H

Hash House a Go Go 61
Hot n Juicy Crawfish 94
House of Blues Gospel Brunch 28

I

Il Fornaio Bakery & Cafe 32

J

Jaburrito 35
Jean Philippe Patisserie 24
Joël Robuchon 60

L

La Cave 58
La Comida 105, 112
Le Village Buffet 62
Lindo Michoacan 86
Lotus of Siam 85

M

Milo's Cellar 122
Mon Ami Gabi 42
Morimoto 60

N

N9NE 96
New York Pizzeria 31
Nobu 63

P

Park on Fremont 104
Peppermill 59-60
Ping Pang Pong 96
Pink Taco 78

R

Rainbow's End Cafe 84
Raku 91

Ramen-ya Katana 58
Restaurant Guy Savoy 60-1
Rivea 62

S

Searsucker Las Vegas 59
Spice Market Buffet 64
Stripsteak 63
Sushisamba 45
SW Steakhouse 50

T

Tacos El Gordo 58
Todd English's Olives 6[?]
Top of the World 62
Twist by Pierre Gagnaire 38

U

Umami Burger 57-8

V

Veggie Delight 94
Vickie's Diner 107
Virgil's Real BBQ 35

W

Wicked Spoon Buffet 6[?]

🍸 Drinking

1

107 SkyLounge 66

B

Bar at Times Square 31
Bastille on 3rd 107
Beauty Bar 105
Beer Park (by Budweiser) 41

C

enter Bar 57
handelier Lounge 68
hateau Nightclub &
    Gardens 42
ommonwealth 105

D

orsey 45
ouble Down Saloon 86
owntown Cocktail
    Room 114
rai's Beachclub &
    Nightclub 67

E

ncore Beach Club 67

F

ireside Lounge 66
lair Nightclub 86
oundation Room 28
rankie's Tiki Room 97
reezone 87

G

arage 86
hostbar 96-7
old Spike 106-7

H

akkasan 64
ofbräuhaus 86
yde 23

I

ntrigue 50

J

ewel 65

M

Mandarin Bar & Tea
    Lounge 68
Marquee 65
Minus5 Ice Bar 27

N

Napoleon's Dueling
    Pianos 42
Nine Fine Irish-
    men 31-2

O

Omnia 65

P

Parasol Up & Parasol
    Down 50
Petrossian Bar 23
Piranha 86-7
Pour 24 32

R

ReBAR 107, 114
Rhumbar 126

S

Skyfall Lounge 27
Surrender 66

T

Todd English P.U.B. 38
Triple 7 114

V

Velveteen Rabbit
    107, 113
VooDoo Rooftop
    Nightclub 97

W

Wet Republic 66

X

XS 66

Entertainment

Beatles LOVE 68
Blue Man Group 68
Brooklyn Bowl 35
Carrot Top 70
Colosseum 70
*Criss Angel Mindfreak
    Live* 70
Fremont Country
    Club 105
House of Blues 28
Joint 87
Kà 54
Le Cabaret 42
Le Rêve the Dream
    49-50
'O' 24
Mandalay Bay Events
    Center 28
MGM Grand Garden
    Arena 54
*Michael Jackson
    ONE* 28
Monte Carlo's 70
Park Theater 70
Pearl 97
Penn & Teller 97
Sapphire 84
Smith Center for the
    Performing Arts
    114-15
T-Mobile Arena 70

World Series of
    Poker 94
Zumanity 32

Shopping

Bonanza Gift Shop 73
Buffalo Exchange
    107, 115
Chinatown Plaza 96
Commercial Center 87
Cosmopolitan 72
Downtown
    Summerlin 133
Fashion Show 71
Gamblers General
    Store 115
Grand Canal Shoppes
    at the Palazzo 46
Grand Canal Shoppes
    at the Venetian 46
Houdini's Magic
    Shop 73
Inyo Fine Cannabis
    Dispensary 87
Las Vegas Premium
    Outlets North 143
Miracle Mile Shops 72
Polaroid Fotobar 35
Rainbow Feather Dyeing
    Co 107, 115
Shoppes at Mandalay
    Place 27
Shops at Cosmopol-
    itan 72
Shops at Crystals 37, 71
Shops at Forum 72
Williams Costume
    Company 115

Our Writers

Andrea Schulte-Peevers

Born and raised in Germany and educated in London and at UCLA, Andrea has travelled the distance to the moon and back in her visits to some 75 countries. She has earned her living as a professional travel writer for over two decades and authored or contributed to nearly 100 Lonely Planet titles as well as to newspapers, magazines and websites. She also works as a travel consultant, translator and editor. Andrea specialises in Germany, Dubai and the UAE, Crete and the Caribbean Islands. She lives in Berlin.

Benedict Walker

Ben was born in Newcastle (NSW, Australia) and grew up in the 'burbs, spending weekends and long summers by the beach. Although he's drawn magnetically to the kinds of mountains he encountered in the Canadian Rockies and the Japanese and Swiss Alps, beach life is in his blood. A fluent Japanese speaker, his first book for LP was *Japan*, and he has since written on Australia, Canada, Germany, Vietnam and the USA. Find him on Instagram @wordsandjourneys.

Published by Lonely Planet Global Limited
CRN 554153
5th edition – December 2017
ISBN 978 1 78657 246 2
© Lonely Planet 2017 Photographs © as indicated 2017
10 9 8 7 6 5 4 3 2 1
Printed in Malaysia